More Praise for Star Sisters

"An excellent book about dealing with the loss of a loved one. Linda Zlotnick fits astrology into the narrative in a way that is easy for the lay person to understand and shows how astrology can have an important role in health and healing."

—ARLAN WISE, former president and current vice president of the Organization for Professional Astrology

"An intricate and nuanced portrait of twin living and losing. Twin loss is an under-researched and under-resourced topic. When I lost my own twin, Bob, at the age of thirty-one to HIV, Linda's book would have been just what I needed at the time to understand the complexity of my grief and to know I was not alone."

—BETH ZEMSKY, MAEd, LICSW, intercultural organizational development consultant and (always) Bob's twin

Star Sisters

An Astrologer's Memoir of Twin Loss

Linda "Moonrabbit" Zlotnick

MOON
RABBIT
PRESS

Star Sisters: An Astrologer's Memoir of Twin Loss
Published by Moonrabbit Press, St. Paul, MN

Paperback ISBN 978-0-578-50376-9
E-book ISBN 978-0-578-50378-3

Publishing consultant: Beth Wright, Wright for Writers LLC
Cover designer: Christian Fuenfhausen

AUTHOR'S NOTE

I have written about people, events, and places as I remember them, using some artistic license. Names of clients and some other people have been changed to protect their privacy.

For Lou Ann, whose memory has become a blessing

**

Perhaps they are not stars, but rather openings
in heaven where the love of our lost ones pours
through and shines upon us to let us know they
are happy.

—INUIT PROVERB

Prologue

Lou Ann is gone. I knew for months she would die, and yet I am shattered. I said goodbye to her one morning as we curled together side by side in her lavender-scented home-hospital bed. She said, "Promise me you'll be okay after I'm gone." There was heartbreak in her clear blue eyes. I lied and said yes. She was close to death at that point; her frail cancer-ravished body having consumed only ice chips for five days. But she was present enough to say goodbye. To worry about me.

Soon after that she left in stages. First her eyes glazed over, her mind gone to the place of golden light, but she maintained regular breathing and heartbeat. Then her hands and feet turned to ice, but still the dependable breathing continued. I held onto that sound as if it were a lifeline. When her breathing became erratic, I knew the end was near. I put my hand on her heart, and as long as I felt it beat, our connection was there.

Then her heart stopped. Not only her heart but our connection. It flew out an open window. This thing I had known from inside our mother's womb. A thin electrical thread of energy, of consciousness, had been cut. I was alone. Totally alone. For the first time. Ever.

It was the aloneness that threatened to destroy me. It pulled me into a hollow blackness, sucked the life from me, and left me breathless and quivering with unspoken fright. Who was I now? Would I ever feel whole again? Did I have enough *me* to survive?

I searched everywhere for the connection. It wasn't in pictures or home videos, although those did remind me of her. It wasn't in her home or in the people who knew her either. That added to my sadness. I imagined being with her, floating above everything and watching, but the emptiness persisted. She floated only in my imagination.

Before falling asleep I asked her to visit me in dreams. At first, nothing. Then came dreams of the back of Lou Ann's head disappearing into a crowd. I was never fast enough to catch anything but a glimpse. I awoke with fury burning through me. How could she be so close and still gone?

I'd never known it was the connection, that thin thread, that mattered. I'd thought it was the person, the twin so like me yet totally herself: the brilliant mind, the dear friend, the keeper of memories, the flesh and blood of her.

A year and two months later I receive an early birthday present: we visit during a dream. Lou Ann is back, in another realm, but we are together. We speak, I cry, she listens and explains. The thread strums again.

Part One
The Shared Path

**

You were born together, and together you shall
be forevermore but let there be spaces in your
togetherness. And let the winds of heaven dance
between you.

—KAHLIL GIBRAN

1

A New Horoscope

When Lou Ann, my identical twin, breathed her final breath, I remember looking at my watch. The time, 1:05 p.m., seared itself onto my brain along with the image of her pale, shrunken body. Knowing the exact timing of things meant everything to me as a lifelong astrologer. Days passed before I could stop the wailing gulps of grief, let alone look up the position of the planets and zodiac.

It wasn't that I didn't want to know; I'd been so curious about my newborn child's birth chart nine years earlier, I left my partner Mindy's bedside as soon as both she and the baby fell asleep and rushed to my computer. But Lou Ann's death was different. We were almost the same person, and now she'd just died. As babies we'd shared a crib, as kids, a stick of gum, a bedroom, clothes, friends, and our deepest feelings. We knew each other the way no one else ever could—well enough that sometimes we didn't even need to talk. As adults, we'd worked hard to live our own lives as individuals, always knowing our bond was special. Was there enough of me left to understand what the planets might say?

Days passed, the raw shock subsiding slowly, until I knew I had to look. "I'm going to my office," I told Mindy that morning, putting my glass in the sink. As bereft as I was, Mindy's support had felt like a tangible thing, like a leg or back brace, during the weeklong shiva, the period of Jewish mourning that we were observing. Shiva was over, and this was something I had to do on my own.

Minutes later, I sat in front of my office computer. Here was where I saw clients, read horoscopes, and studied the ephemeris, a book listing the positions of the planets. My practice was successful, a solid presence in our lives, and my client appointments reached into the coming weeks. I loved my office, my sanctuary, and that day I felt relieved that the intense heat and humidity of high summer had finally abated. The cooler air through the open window helped to lift the underwater feeling of grief. For the last thirty years, looking at the stars helped me understand every aspect of life. Would it now?

I had never run a death chart. A computerized form did not exist. Instead, I used the form for a birth chart and entered Lou Ann's date, place, and time of death. Certainly I had studied the heavens after my mom died, but not in this exact way. The screen blurred, making me blink as I typed numbers and letters. After the wheel popped up, I realized my cheeks were wet. I took a deep breath, grabbed a Kleenex, wiped my face, and looked.

I was stunned. It appeared the same as every other chart I'd seen. Somehow, I expected a chart that would show the exit from life in a different way than its entrance. Then it hit me. I had to get home and talk to Mindy.

I found her in the kitchen, washing dishes. Our children, Ana and Della, were upstairs playing. The radio was playing something soulful and soft, and Mindy turned as I rushed in, alarm on her face. "What is it?"

I threw the chart onto the kitchen table. "Life and death are bound together," I said. I knew I was speaking too loudly and lowered my voice. Our household had just found its peaceful center again, and I didn't want to disturb the peace. Mindy waited. I took a deep breath to calm myself, trying to put my realization into words.

"Just because Lou Ann's bright flame was extinguished doesn't mean all life ended." I lifted the paper copy of the chart in front of us. "Look," I said, pointing to Saturn, "Lou Ann died at the exact beginning of our second Saturn Return." A Saturn Return we shared as identical twins. A momentous event in my life during its first passage, and in the charts of my clients. Saturn influenced life purpose, life lessons, and how we find meaning. "This shows I'm about to start a new path."

"So her death was tied to your destiny?" Mindy had studied astrology for a couple years after college. She knew what this meant.

"Yeah." I took her hand, led her to the living room, and we sank onto the couch. "I know there are lessons, important ones, for me to learn from this." I took a deep breath. "From her death."

She leaned in close. "You mean besides how to live without her?"

"That's a big one, yes." I secretly wondered if I was capable of meeting the challenge, but I forged ahead. "Saturn is about self-responsibility, internalizing my own authority. I always counted on Lou Ann, sometimes too much. I think I need to grow up more, find who I am without her."

I thought back to how surprised my parents had been when they found out they were having twins. "We didn't even have a name for you, Linda," my dad once told me. "We assumed we were having one baby until your mother's eight-month check-up when the doctor heard two distinct heart beats."

"Did twins run in either family?" Lou Ann had asked him.

He shook his head. "Your mother was upset. We'd only bought one crib and baby clothes for one."

I'd begun studying astrology by then but kept my interest to myself, knowing my father wouldn't understand. He'd given us our birth certificates that day, and I held tight to mine, as if it were a prize. Having our birth times would allow me to calculate our charts. Lou Ann was born first, at 5:23 p.m., weighing five pounds two ounces. She was followed by me, the unexpected twin, at 5:47 p.m., weighing four pounds eleven ounces.

No one knew yet how important those two times would become to me, the twin who would become a professional astrologer. What they did know was my low birth weight meant I must go to the incubator. Away from Lou Ann and from Mom. Alone.

Like many twins, we were born premature. When, as an adult, I heard about the days I spent in the incubator, isolated and untouched, it was almost as if they happened to someone else. In 1948 incubators were lonely places where only feeding and changing took place but my body remembered the isolation on a cellular level. After I became a mom, I imagined all the love and attention Lou Ann enjoyed as a singleton, and the chaos I brought, not only as a second baby, but a sickly one at that. It made sense that as a teen, and until mid-life, I struggled with irrational feelings of abandonment and inadequacy. As the smaller, sicker twin, I had no way of knowing that the twenty-four minutes of difference in our birth time would make all the difference in our lifespan. I didn't know what was written in the stars for either of us. All of that knowing came later.

2

A Shared Crib

For our first four years, we lived in a tiny one-bedroom apartment just off Lake Street and Minnehaha Avenue in south Minneapolis. I remember hearing my parents talk about the close quarters where Lou Ann and I shared a crib, and then a twin bed in a room that was supposed to be a closet. Money was scarce. Dad worked as a cashier at a small grocery store across the alley, and Mom stayed home like most women in those early years after World War II.

One hot summer day when we were almost four years old, Lou Ann and I were alone in the backyard collecting rocks from under the clothesline and putting them into small piles.

"Let's go visit Daddy," Lou Ann said.

I shook my head no. Mom had told us to stay in the yard and I already knew not to make her mad. The sound of insects buzzing grew louder in my ears while the sun burned the back of my arms and neck. Lou Ann grabbed my hand and smiled. I shook my head no again, even as she pulled me to my feet. Her hand in mine made it easier to be courageous and follow her. Then she smiled a big, bright smile and said, "It'll be fun. C'mon." I changed my mind. I wanted to go.

She pushed open the gate to the alley and we ran fast. By the count of four, five, six, we were at the store. As the door opened, big fans whirred coolness onto my face and arms. Instantly, I felt much better. Dad stood behind the counter, looking handsome in his big white shirt and apron with his jet black hair. "What a nice surprise, girls!" Smiling, he leaned down to hug us. He smelled like Brylcreem and Old Spice. "You two came here by yourselves?"

"We ran all the way," Lou Ann said, still holding my hand.

"Mom will be worried." He picked up Lou Ann, then me. "You two sit here on the counter while I call home."

Those minutes before Mom arrived were some of the most delicious moments I'd known. My legs swung in tandem with Lou Ann's in the cool air. Dad called his coworkers over to see us. "These are my twin daughters, Lou Ann and Linda Lea." Mom had dressed us in matching blue and white seersucker sundresses and braided our shiny light brown hair into two perfect braids each. The grownups said "so cute," "how adorable," and "aren't they sweet?" as they smiled and patted our heads. After they left, Lou Ann smiled at me, her blue eyes twinkling, as we dangled our legs in perfect unison—hers, as always, a little longer than mine.

Dad brought us a Popsicle in a white wrapper. He broke it in half against the counter and then unwrapped it. We each took one stick. I sucked in the sweet juice and felt the coolness run down my throat. It was orange, our favorite flavor. I knew then, sitting up high in the cool air, getting a treat with an adult's attention, that we'd done something naughty. I didn't care; I could feel my heart smiling. My sister was full of great ideas.

I remembered a few weeks earlier when we played outside with the neighbor boy who was visiting his grandparents. We were all tired of playing tag when he'd asked us to pull down our underpants and in return he'd show us his pee-pee. I was scared, knowing that showing private parts was wrong, but after Lou Ann went ahead, I did the same. Moments later, Mom ran into the yard, hair flying out of her scarf, screaming at him to leave. We were sent to bed without dinner. When I complained about being hungry, Lou Ann told me she would do it again because boy's privates were so ugly. We giggled so hard I forgot about my empty stomach.

As we ate our Popsicles, Mom came in. "You girls all right?" Her voice was loud and her face was mad. "I told you to stay in the yard!" The grocery store door slammed hard behind her.

"They just came to visit me at work, honey." Dad put his hand on her shoulder.

Shaking his hand off and dropping her voice low, Mom said, "Something terrible could have happened to them."

Lou Ann kept swinging her legs, a hint of a smile on her face, so I did too.

"They're fine, Dee." Dad used his nickname for her. "They're just being kids."

I hurried to finish my last bite of Popsicle and so did Lou Ann.

"Time to go, girls." Mom turned around, grabbed us each by an arm, and yanked us off the counter. Popsicle sticks went flying. As I sailed off the counter, it seemed I floated above my own head. People turned around to look as she pulled us outside.

On the other side of the door in the alley, she stopped and leaned her face close to ours. "You do not disobey me, understand?" Her face was red and her fingers hurt my arm. "You're both getting spankings as soon as we get home." I dragged my feet but we were home in seven, eight, nine, ten. We walked into the kitchen. "Lean over and pull down your underpants, Lou Ann." Mom's voice was hard as she held a brown wooden spoon in her hand. "Remember, this hurts me more than it hurts you," she said, giving Lou Ann three hard smacks. "I told you to stay in the yard." Lou Ann stood up, her mouth a thin line. She yanked up her pants and studied the floor. "Now you, Linda." My legs trembled as I struggled to pull down my elastic waistband, my heart beating fast. I got my pants down to my ankles and touched my toes the way we'd been taught. The sweet taste of orange Popsicle stayed on my tongue until the first hit.

Two years later, Dad got a new job, and we moved to a bigger house on Oliver Avenue, where, in the fall, we started elementary school. We had a bedroom in the attic with paneling on the walls and carpeting on the floor. On the way to our room was a long hall, big enough to fit a crib for our new baby brother, Mark, when he arrived. Lou Ann couldn't wait until we'd have a room all to ourselves, but all I could think about was how fun it would be to have a baby brother.

**

The screen door slammed behind me as I followed Lou Ann into the kitchen. A glass pan of brownies sat cooling on top of the stove. The rich, sweet chocolate smell made my mouth water and I almost forgot about the report card in my pocket. Second grade had just ended, and Lou Ann was already across the room, talking to Mom, handing her a paper as she stood at the ironing board. There were piles of laundry in a basket on the floor and more on the table behind her. Since Mark was born and we'd moved to the new house, she was even busier with feeding him, washing clothes, and ironing. Having a baby brother was no fun at all.

"Linda, give me your report card right now." I pulled myself away from smelling the brownies and took the sweaty envelope out of my jacket pocket, stumbling a bit as I walked across the threshold to where Mom stood. I'd seen the one B on the way home and knew I was in for a tongue-lashing.

"There's a B here, Linda." She stared at me. "Are you stupid?"

I felt myself cringe inside. Of course I was stupid compared to Lou Ann, who got straight As. I looked at my twin. She just barely shook her head, mouthing the word no. Mom's wrath poured over me and leaked inside, but I knew what I had to do.

"No, Mom." I looked at the floor.

"I can't tell you two how many times I wished I'd had more schooling. You have no idea how lucky you are, living in this house, going to that school." She cleared her throat. "Look at me, Linda." Mom's eyes were hard. "Is your identical twin sister smarter than you?" She paused, waiting, then said, "Answer me."

The words stuck in my throat: "She's not." But I didn't believe it.

"Linda, go in the kitchen and put two brownies on plates: one for me and one for your sister. When you get all As you can have a brownie."

As I turned and walked into the kitchen, I clenched my fists tight. I liked the pinch of fingernails against my palm. As I put brownies on plates for Mom and Lou Ann, I snuck a big crumb from the pan into my mouth and chewed. It tasted sweet.

3

Castor and Pollux

Lou Ann and I were just about to turn eleven when my view of the world changed in two major ways. At the end of fourth grade I learned Lou Ann and I shared a special gift called ESP, and over that summer I discovered more about my deep connection to the stars.

Lou Ann handed me the pile of square cards we'd cut from the magazine section of the Sunday *Tribune* that said, "Test Your ESP!" There were five cards with symbols on them: a square, a circle, a cross, a star, and a wave. The test was for one person to concentrate on projecting the image and for the other person to guess. The magazine section included a score card and said to use an egg timer for all five cards, so I'd found one in the kitchen. The house was quiet; Mom and Dad had taken Mark shopping. I looked at the first card, a circle, and imagined sending the picture to Lou Ann.

"It's a circle," she said right away. I turned over another card, and there was a square. She got that one too. We played twice, and she got eight out of ten correct. We beat the timer by a lot.

"I guess we have ESP," Lou Ann said, checking the rules before we tried it again, this time with me guessing. It shouldn't have been such a big surprise since we often finished each other's sentences or had the same ideas, but the words "extra sensory perception" made it more real.

The next day at school, everyone was talking about taking the ESP test and failing miserably. Suddenly we were celebrities among our friends and classmates; we were the twins who could read each other's minds.

**

As a young child I'd loved the stars, but they were hard to see from our family's home in the middle of south Minneapolis. My earliest memory of real stargazing happened on Devil's Lake, just outside Webster, Wisconsin, during the summer before fifth grade.

It was the last night of two glorious weeks of summer camp, and our entire group of ten-year-old girls planned to break curfew. As soon as the counselors left for their meeting, all twelve of us rushed out the narrow cabin door. Over the tops of the trees, the moon was setting, but there was still enough brightness to see the path that led down to the lake.

I was frightened, worried about getting in trouble, until Lou Ann squeezed my hand. "The counselors won't be back for another thirty minutes," she said, blue eyes sparkling in the moonlight. Her excitement was contagious, and I knew she was right. "Race you to the lake." She broke into a run, golden brown hair streaming behind her, legs flashing white against the dark ground. The night sounds of croaking frogs and the long grass muffled our footfalls as we sped down the path. Just as I got a second wind and closed in on her, the lake glistened directly in front of us. We both slowed.

"Here," she said, plopping down. The sand was still warm from the day. It felt good under my bare feet as I settled next to her. Lou Ann shifted closer and leaned into my left side. We both looked up at the bright night sky spilling over with stars. I'd never seen a sky like this before and I wanted to stay there, gazing upward, forever.

"See that?" I pointed toward the north. "The W? That's Cassiopeia."

Already I knew some of the constellations. In fourth grade we had studied astronomy, and I'd fallen in love with it. Every piece of the sky we studied stuck in my brain without effort. On our weekly trips to the library, I searched for more books about the stars and planets, absorbing everything I could, checking out my limit of books.

"I count five." My sister leaned in further, and I felt the comfort of her warm body against mine. "One for . . ."

". . . for each person in our family." We finished together.

I heard a splash. Circular ripples spread out in front of us, barely visible in the dark. "Sis, did you see the jumping fish?" I asked.

"No." She was looking at the sky again. "What's the rectangle over there with the two bright stars?"

"Castor and Pollux, the twins." A warm breeze blew across my bare shoulders and face; it smelled like sweet clover. "They were wild horse tamers." We sat in silence for a moment, and I searched back in my memory for the stories I'd read about the sky. "I think one of them gave up his immortality so they wouldn't have to be apart."

A loon sounded its mournful song, then moments later another bird returned the call.

"I'd do that for you, in a heartbeat," Lou Ann said. She jumped to her feet. "Last one back to the cabin is a rotten egg."

I didn't know then how important Lou Ann's promise would be, and how themes of mortality and unity would weave themselves into our lives. Instead, I took Lou Ann for granted, particularly during those two special weeks spent together at summer camp. We went each summer for five years, until we were too old to be campers.

The summer before our senior year of high school, I'd already committed to a full-time summer job when Lou Ann told me she'd been accepted as a counselor at our beloved Herzl Camp.

"Wait, I want to be a counselor too," I said. "And you'll be gone for eight weeks."

She'd called me into our beige bedroom with its two high windows, empty walls, and beige bedspreads and closed the door behind her. Mom was slowly redecorating our new house, but she hadn't started on our bedroom. Lou Ann sat on her twin bed. I stood in front of her, hands on hips.

"I never thought they'd hire me," she said.

"That's not the point, and you know it." My fingernails bit into my palms.

Lou Ann looked at the floor. "Mom's driving me crazy, bossing us around, treating us like babies. Sometimes I need to be away from this family, even you. It's easier to be myself when we're apart." She sighed. "I'll write every day. I promise."

Just weeks earlier, Lou Ann had told me she wanted her own friends, and now she wanted to get away, even from me. This had never happened before. A weight settled over my chest. "Mom drives me crazy too," I said. "What will I do without you?"

There was a long silence. "I still love you, you know." Lou Ann's eyes were soft. "But we have to grow up sometime, and that means having lives of our own." She sighed. "I'm ready now."

My fists unclenched and I sat down next to Lou Ann on the bed. She leaned into my left side and, as I took a deep breath, I remembered the two stars we saw every year at camp, Castor and Pollux, and Lou Ann's heartfelt promise.

"I'll kill you if you don't write every day," I said, hitting her arm. Then I left the room, pulling the door closed behind me.

4
Abandoned

The back door shuddered in the wind as Dad yanked it closed. He moved slowly to a kitchen chair and slumped into it, still wearing his coat and boots. Mom got mad at anyone who wore boots in the house, even more when it was snowing like today, so I waited for him to shuck them off and apologize to someone, but he didn't. "Girls, Mark, come here," he said. His voice sounded like a stranger's. "I have something to tell you."

My heart pounded hard in my chest, like it wanted to escape, as Lou Ann and I walked to the kitchen table. Something was really wrong. Something with Mom. Without thinking I moved my chair closer to my twin's. Ten-year-old Mark sat down next to Dad.

The kitchen windows rattled in their frames as the wind gusted outside. When Dad looked up, his eyes were bloodshot and his face was wet with tears. "There's no easy way to tell you this." He ran his hands through his thick black hair. "Your mother just died. I was with her when she stopped breathing." He put his hands over his face, and when he sobbed his entire body moved up and down. "Dear God, what will I do now?"

I'd never seen him cry before, not in all of my seventeen years. I looked at Lou Ann and saw that her face was pale and frozen. Dad collapsed onto the table and his crying got louder. It started a sharp noise in my head and a burning in the back of my throat.

Without knowing what I was doing, I pushed away from the table and ran to the bathroom. A mix of cold toilet water and vomit splashed my face and I let it all go. When I was finished, I grabbed a tissue and wiped my face. The bathroom spun around and I leaned my head against the cool tiles. Mom had cancer, she wasn't dead. Dad had promised us she'd be fine; she'd be home soon.

There was a frantic pounding on the door.

"Go away," I yelled, "I'm sick."

The door burst open and Lou Ann heaved into the sink. The room filled with the smell of tuna fish vomit. I gagged and grabbed the waste basket. Once everything had poured from my body, I could still hear Dad sobbing in the kitchen. I dragged myself down the hall to our bedroom and fell on my bed. A minute or two later I heard Lou Ann come in. I wanted to run over and curl up next to her like we always did when we were scared, but something had changed. She felt remote, surrounded by a brittle shell, out of reach.

Time passed in that silent bedroom until it seemed as if I'd been lying on my tear-stained pillow for days. I could hear Mark crying and Dad talking on the phone. I didn't know what to do. Usually we did whatever Mom told us. It was only a couple years ago that she stopped setting out our school clothes, double-checking that we'd done our homework, and telling us what we were allowed to do with our free time. What would life be like without her? Many times when she ridiculed me, or when I had to miss something fun to stay home and take care of her, I wished that she would just die. I felt terrible. Did my wishing make her die? I looked over at Lou Ann again, but her face was turned against the wall. She never lay that way; we always slept facing each other.

There was a quick knock on the door and Dad walked in. His face was solemn now, composed. He looked at my puffy eyes, and then over at Lou Ann. "No one here is feeling sorry for themselves," he said. "Your brother and I need you to be strong." His voice was cold. "Go wash your face and put on something nice. People are coming for shiva in twenty minutes."

Shiva meant it was all true. Mom was dead.

What I didn't know then was that, by the time Mom's cancer was diagnosed, it had already moved into her lungs and liver. I didn't know until later she had ignored her symptoms for a long time, letting the cancer spread. Even if she'd gone to the doctor earlier, I'm not certain cancer treatment in 1965 was advanced enough to cure her.

My father left the room, closing our door. I waited for Lou Ann to get up, but she didn't move. So I pushed myself off the bed and went back to the bathroom, which still smelled of vomit and misery. I ran the water in the sink until it was warm, found a washcloth, and began cleaning my face, neck, and arms, scrubbing hard. I brushed my teeth and hair. Then I went back to our bedroom and found something to wear.

Shiva meant relatives, family friends, people from the synagogue, the rabbi. I needed to look presentable, as if I weren't falling apart. Everyone, not just Dad, would want me to be strong.

Finally, Lou Ann gave a huge sigh and turned over, sitting up. She rubbed her face and our eyes met. "These last weeks, all I thought about was how much better life would be if she died." Then she looked away. Something broke apart inside me as a steely mask descended over her face. I didn't know then that part of what we were feeling was called survivors' guilt, and our family had a long legacy of it.

On the living room couch I crossed my legs at the ankle the way I was taught: "You always want to look and act like a lady." I heard echoes of Mom's voice in my head as I looked down at the white living room rug. Dad had forgotten to take the plastic cover off the couch and chairs the way Mom always did for company, and my legs stuck to the plastic. Mark sat next to me, his face pale against his white dress shirt. On my other side sat Lou Ann, wearing one of our pleated wool skirts, a matching sweater, nylons, and dress shoes. She seemed to be frozen in place while Mark fidgeted constantly. Someone nearby smelled like stinky cigars.

The doorbell rang and Dad opened the door. A blast of icy air pushed in through the opening.

"Rabbi, come in," Dad said. People talked and shifted around, and then I heard the rabbi's high, nasally voice as I watched my distorted reflection in his shiny black shoes.

"*Baruch Hashem*," he said. "It was God's will that your mother was taken, and starting now you must honor her memory. Starting today you will say kaddish for her for seven days and every Sabbath for a year. This is a sacred responsibility." He dug into an embroidered bag where he kept his prayer shawl and pulled out four torn black ribbons. "Pete, come join us for *kriah*."

Dad stood next to Mark, Lou Ann, and me. He bowed his head. I bowed mine too. When the prayer ended, the rabbi handed each of us a ribbon and a safety pin. "You are required to wear this for one month to honor your wife and mother." The rabbi looked at each of us. "It will show people you are in mourning." I took the pin, and when I opened it, I accidentally poked my thumb. The blood tasted like rust.

5

Covered Mirrors

A towel covered the bathroom mirror the next day; my father had put it there as a sign that our family was in mourning. It wasn't just a dream. Mom was dead. Just last week I was bringing her apple juice, sitting on the side of her bed, and telling her about my humanities class. I grabbed onto the sink and turned on the cold water. Splashing my face hurt but it drove the dizziness and tears away.

For the seven days of shiva there would be no radio, TV, or reading—only prayer and remembering. I never thought the rules of shiva would apply to me.

Aunt Pearl and Aunt Eva talked in hushed tones in our kitchen as they plated the food that people brought. I heard the percolator bubbling on the stove and smelled fresh coffee. Breakfast. I didn't feel like eating.

"Lou Ann. Linda. Come sit down, girls," Aunt Eva called. "Want some eggs?"

"No thanks," I said, stopping outside the kitchen doorway, not wanting to get closer to those smells. My body was quivering; I might throw up again any minute.

"What's happening next?" Lou Ann asked, moving in close beside me. I could feel the heat from her skin.

"The rabbi will be here in an hour to say kaddish and the funeral is this afternoon." Aunt Eva had shadows under her eyes. "You better eat something."

"Not hungry," Lou Ann said. She grabbed my hand, and we walked down the hall to our room.

She closed the door tight, then plopped on her bed. I sat next to her. "You know what I just remembered?" she said. "Mom throwing up so loud in the night it woke me up."

I looked over at her. Her face was pinched.

"You know, the night before she went back to the hospital. I heard her tell Dad she didn't want to die."

"She knew?" I felt my eyes start to burn and water. "Why didn't Dad tell us?"

Someone knocked and then opened the bedroom door. Aunt Dianne walked in. We loved Aunt Dianne. She was always so kind, fun, and she was an identical twin herself. She'd married Dad's brother and was radically different from Mom, laughing loud and often, and not seeming to care what other people thought. She held her arms open wide as tears ran down her cheeks. "You poor, sweet girls." She pulled me into a warm hug, and then Lou Ann too.

"I don't want to go to the funeral." Lou Ann pulled away and wiped her face with both hands.

I didn't either, but I didn't want to say it. "Do we have to?" I asked instead.

"Yes, you do," our aunt said. We waited. She sighed. "I can't tell you how sorry I am about your mother. She expected a lot from you, probably too much, but she loved you."-

"I can't stop crying," I said, walking to the nightstand for a tissue.

"Cry then, but put on a skirt and a blouse," she said. "The rabbi will want to talk to you."

THE CHAIRS IN the funeral parlor were hard, and I didn't know how to act. We'd been told to dress up and not cry. That's all. At least I'd managed to stay away from the open casket when Dad grabbed Lou Ann and Mark to take them up there. I didn't want to see Mom like that. When I closed my eyes, I could barely remember how she looked when she had hair and wasn't so thin that every bone showed.

The rabbi began the service. When he talked about Mom, he used words like "devoted mother" and "loving wife." The room swirled as I felt myself pulled in every direction, remembering my mother in very different ways. How hard she hit us, how she hurt me with her words, how awful she made me feel. But I found if I bit the insides of my cheeks I could sit still and listen, stifle the urge to speak and the urge to cry.

THE ICY WIND whipped through my nylon stockings and up my dress coat the moment I got out of the car at the snowy cemetery. I felt my entire body shiver as Dad led us to a big black hole where they would lower Mom's coffin. It loomed on the ground with the ropes already attached. I found it hard to breathe. The rabbi waved us over. He quickly gathered the required group of ten men and began to chant from a small black prayer book. We stood and shivered.

"*Yitgadal v'yitkadash, sh'mei raba . . .*" I looked around at the headstones with familiar Jewish names on them. Names of people from our synagogue. Dead people. Mom didn't belong here. Neither did we. All the families we knew had two parents, both alive. What would we do now? Dad worked all the time and Mom had made all our decisions for us.

"Sis," Lou Ann whispered, nudging me with her elbow. "Grab some dirt." She motioned to the pile. I reached down with my glove. The dirt was icy, bits of frost clinging to it. Mine was the third handful to hit the coffin. The sound it made was dull, like the throb in the back of my throat. At that moment it seemed my throat would hurt for the rest of my life.

The car ride home and the days of people coming for shiva blurred into a long, heavy mess, just like the snow that weighted the trees and choked the streets.

* *

Shiva was finally over, and we were back in school. Most days, at least for a while, when I got home I just pretended Mom was in the hospital. It seemed easier that way. Lou Ann and I would sit at the kitchen table with Mark, all doing homework. We'd put some chicken and potatoes in the oven to roast for dinner. This had been our normal life since Mom had gotten sick.

"You're all grown up now and I expect you to take over," Dad told us the day after the funeral.

I got used to it, but all of the changes seemed to be taking a heavy toll on my twin.

"What stinks like cigarettes?" I asked one day, walking into the house an hour after school ended.

Lou Ann sat at the kitchen table, flicking ashes from a cigarette into a big glass ashtray.

"Mom would be mad if she caught you smoking in the house," I said. "Besides, why are you smoking?" It was all I could do to stop from turning around and walking back to our neighbor Anne's house, where I'd been eating fresh-baked raisin oatmeal cookies with her and her two young daughters. The smoke hurt my eyes. I yanked open the kitchen window, letting in a blast of cold air.

"Well, Mom isn't here, is she?" Lou Ann's eyes filled with rage. "And Mark is such a fucking brat," she said, grinding out the cigarette. "I told him to start on his homework and he started crying."

We'd decided to take turns coming right home from school to take care of Mark. Part of me agreed with Lou Ann. Mark was a brat. He wasn't the only one whose mother died, but he cried over every little thing as if he was. Sometimes I wondered, though: if I'd been a better daughter, less selfish and more thoughtful the way Mom always said I should be, would she still be alive?

Later, Lou Ann and I danced together, singing along with Diana Ross in our basement family room. Dancing was our reward for folding yet another load of laundry after making dinner and doing the dishes.

"Baby, baby, baby, where did our love go? Don't you want me? Don't you want me no more?" The Supremes' number one hit song filled the air as the black 45 rpm record circled round and round on the phonograph.

After a while, I didn't feel like dancing anymore, but across from me on the dark patterned linoleum floor Lou Ann stomped to the four-four beat. Her black and white saddle shoes thumped and whacked the floor. As Diana sang the chorus, Lou Ann got louder and fiercer, feet pounding on the floor like she was beating back a flood.

THE PHONE RANG, and I picked it up.

"Hello, this is Linda Lea Zlotnick speaking," I said. Mom had insisted we answer the phone politely.

"I'd like to speak to your mother," an adult voice said.

A terrible pounding started in my chest. "She isn't home. Can I take a message?"

"When do you expect her?"

"Call back tomorrow." The words tumbled out of my mouth as I hurried to hang up the phone.

Until I moved out of the house two years later, I always answered the same way when someone called and asked for Mom. When I asked Dad for help with this, he just said, "Tell them to call back later," or something else equally unhelpful. It was the same way he responded to a thousand other things. Then he would disappear into his room or into the den to watch TV or read the newspaper. After an evening with more of our questions, he said, "You girls are all grown up now, so you don't have to ask permission about everything." He assumed that the house would stay clean, dinner would appear on the table every night, and the dishes and laundry would be done as usual. We would become the parents, Lou Ann and I, for my brother and father. We would replace Mom.

Eventually we settled into a routine with Mark and Dad, and as time passed a few things happened that I didn't expect. I was relieved to not have Mom controlling every aspect of my life. To not have her yelling at me, berating me and Lou Ann. At first I couldn't shake the feeling that she was still somewhere in the house watching me, judging me, and finding fault. But over time that feeling faded and I started feeling better. Lou Ann and I began to have the social life of normal teenagers, going out with friends and even going to parties—things I didn't know I'd been missing.

6
Hidden Motives

On a Saturday morning a month after shiva ended, our neighbor Anne called, asking if Lou Ann or I could babysit. Eager to get out of our silent, grief-filled house, I said yes. After dinner, I walked over through the cold winter air, looking at the lights in other people's homes, imagining mothers laughing with their children or reading to them before bed. I thought of our house, with my brother Mark holed up in his room, my dad in the den behind his newspaper, and Lou Ann talking on the phone with a friend I didn't know.

When I arrived, Anne greeted me at the door, dressed up for her evening out. Both girls were already in bed and Shel, her husband, had just left. Anne told me to expect one of them home by ten. So I settled in at the kitchen table to catch up on homework. Twenty minutes later, I was surprised to hear the back door open. Shel walked in. "My meeting was cancelled, but you can finish the hour," he said, hanging his coat on a rack by the door. "I'll pay you for the whole time."

I knew Shel and Anne fairly well and liked them both. They were frequent visitors in our home, and one of them had come to Mom's shiva every day, something only close friends usually did. Shel was a lively conversationalist and liked showing us unique things he'd found. Just last week he'd brought over his latest purchase, a gadget that you could strap on your hand to give a wonderful, soothing massage. He tried it out on me and Lou Ann for a couple minutes.

We sat in front of him on our ottoman while he chatted with Dad. The massage felt good on my tight shoulders, but I couldn't figure out why Shel was breathing so fast for most of it. If Dad noticed, he didn't say anything. So I shrugged it off, not even asking Lou Ann if it had happened to her.

Now Shel stood near the table, looking down at me and my homework. I wondered if he wanted to talk about what I was reading in English class, something he often asked about when he visited our house. I looked up to see him pull a comb out of his back pocket and run it through his thick brown hair. He'd played football in college, and sometimes I saw him out the back window throwing a ball around with his buddies. His eyes swept up and down my body.

"Linda," he said slowly, "how about I give you a shoulder massage while we talk about books?"

"I probably should finish this and go," I said, but he had already strapped the massager to his hand. It made a low rumbling noise. I leaned back in the kitchen chair, and he put his hands on my shoulders. At first the touch was soothing. I felt my body relax a little, but then something changed. I tried to move away but realized that might be rude, so I decided to wait another minute. Finally, he stopped. I immediately began gathering my homework into my book bag.

"We just started *The Scarlet Letter* in English class last week," I said, trying to be polite. *It was just a massage*, I scolded myself inside. *You've had them before.* I heard a car backfire on the street and I jumped.

But he wasn't done. Shel began running his hands up and down my arms, and I heard that fast breathing again. It grew louder. I was frozen in the chair. "We're just on chapter two," I mumbled. His hands moved faster. I felt one brush against my breast. I pulled forward in the chair, but his hands pinned me in place. My heart was racing.

"Thanks for the massage," I said. "I better go home. My dad will wonder where I am." My dad wouldn't even notice, but it sounded good. I started to stand up, but Shel pushed me back down into the chair and slid around to face me, propping himself against the table.

His voice was raspy. His breath stank of cigarettes. "You're a selfish girl, Linda. I've watched you with your family. All you do is take and take." He moved his face closer to mine. "Now it's time for you to give."

Mom had always told me I was selfish. She'd said it so often I believed her. "Linda Lea, you never think of anyone else," she'd say to me but never to Lou Ann or Mark. I hadn't understood what she meant. What made a person selfish or not? Wasn't it normal to think of yourself? I looked up at Shel, who was watching me, and decided he must be right too. In that moment of hesitation, he was on me.

He straddled me on the chair, his hands squeezing my breasts. Suddenly his bitter tongue was in my mouth; I gagged, pushing at him, jerking my face away. Nothing had ever prepared me for this. I daydreamed about boys I knew at school—who didn't? But I never imagined a grown-up would do such a disgusting thing. His two girls were asleep upstairs; his wife could come back any minute. But he wasn't stopping. Suddenly I had an idea. "Just let me up to pee," I said. "I gotta go bad."

Amazingly, his weight lifted off me. "Okay, sugar," he said, smiling at me like we were going to have some real fun. "You come right back."

As fast as I'd ever done anything, I snatched up my coat and book bag and dodged around him, out the back door, running across the snowy lawn toward our house. I burst in our back door and raced downstairs to the bathroom just in time for the first wave of vomit to hit the toilet.

When I was empty, I got up, rinsed my face and mouth, and went to my desk in our basement study. I had to write down what happened. I wanted to tell Lou Ann everything, but I couldn't say it out loud. At that thought, cramps shot through my stomach and I ran to the bathroom again.

Lou Ann looked up. "What's wrong with you?" she asked. "Are you sick?"

"This'll explain it," I whispered. I handed her the sheet of paper and watched her read it line by line. Then she grabbed her pen and started to write. Half a page later she handed me the note: *I was worried he would try something last time I was there. He came home early that night, too, and stared at my body, so I made up an excuse and left. I don't think we can tell Dad. He's too sad. I'll help you figure out what to do.*

I looked up from reading. My twin sister opened her arms and I fell into their safety. Lou Ann held me until I stopped shaking. It took eleven years of me forgetting, then remembering, getting mad, and finding a good therapist before I worked out a plan with Lou Ann to confront Shel.

As I talked with the therapist, I remembered the day we asked Mom when we'd be old enough to date. We had just started high school, and lots of girls we knew were dating. Her mouth pulled into a thin line and her back stiffened. She told us we could date when we were high school seniors, but added, with a harsh bitterness in her voice, "Just remember, all men are animals." I didn't believe her, at least not then.

Years later, I found a picture of my mother standing next to her parents. Fleeing the pogroms in Russia, they had settled in Iowa farm country, a place rife with anti-Semitism, but where their big garden and chicken coop could help feed a family of six. I remembered my grandfather as a gruff man, an orthodox Jew who ran a strict home and was given to outbursts of rage. My grandmother, a tiny gray-haired woman, seemed to live in the kitchen and smelled of cinnamon and sugar. Neither of them spoke much English, so Mom had to interpret for us kids when we visited each summer.

In this picture, Mom looked about fourteen years old. Her bangs formed a perfect curl on her forehead. Wearing a dress that was at least one size too large, she stood with her arms wrapped around her body, slightly turned away from both her parents with a distant, haunted look in her eyes. Something about her warning to us, her posture and the look in her eyes, made me wonder if she'd been the victim of her own father, a man who scared me during every visit.

1

A Bridesmaid

Mom always wanted us to be the first in the family to go to college. Lou Ann and I enrolled at the University of Minnesota before high school ended, but too late for Mom to see. "College is where nice girls go to get their Mrs. degree," she'd often said, but I knew I wanted much more than being someone's wife. Lou Ann told me she wanted to get married, and soon, saying it was the only way to escape living at home.

During our second semester, Lou Ann met Joe, the teaching assistant in her algebra class. He was Jewish, three years older, and studying to be a math professor, meeting Mom's criteria for a good husband. Lou Ann told me they clicked instantly, their eyes meeting across a crowded room. It wasn't long before Joe proposed and they set their wedding date.

Aunt Dianne helped Lou Ann pick out a wedding dress with simple, flattering lines and a tasteful tiara for her hair. Her elegance was a far cry from the way I felt in my uncomfortable bridesmaid dress. Every time I moved my arms, the elastic waistband of the dress chafed, and I felt my skin getting raw by the time we walked into the sanctuary for photographs.

"You on the end, move one step to the left. Now everyone, smile." The photographer ordered us around for what seemed like hours. We all stood up straight and tried to look as if we were enjoying ourselves. I was miserable. I was happy for Lou Ann's happiness, but keenly aware of this marker in our lives, the first time we would truly be apart. Shifting my weight from foot to foot, I tried not to feel jealous that Lou Ann was the first twin to find love and get married. She was ahead of me again.

As I stood there, trying not to move my arms, I thought about the ultimatum I'd given Dad the day before the wedding. "You can't make me live at home after Lou Ann gets married," I'd told him. "I've saved money so I'm moving into an apartment on campus." I was sick of cooking and cleaning for him and Mark. But more than that, I knew life would be intolerable at home without Lou Ann.

"Girls, hold your flowers with both hands just above your waists." The photographer's voice was extra loud for us bridesmaids. "That's right. Smile into the camera." I did what he said even though my face ached. "Okay, the last one is just of the twins." As I posed again for the camera, I tried to swallow the hollow feeling climbing up my throat. Lou Ann was about to be married, and I wasn't. My current boyfriend, Scott, had proposed. And although I liked his attention, I wanted to be in love the way Lou Ann was with Joe.

We'd touched up our makeup and hair, and it seemed like a minute later when I heard the wedding music. It was time for me to walk down the aisle as the maid of honor. Scott, wearing a dress suit I'd never seen before, stood waiting for me. I took his arm and we walked to the front of the synagogue. My feet wobbled in my new high-heeled shoes, and I was glad for his steady arm to hold. We found our places at the front.

The music changed to "Here Comes the Bride," and Dad beamed, nodding at people he knew as he and Lou Ann walked down the aisle. Her blue eyes were aglow as she stepped in time to the music, smiling at Joe, who watched her keenly. I couldn't stop looking at my sister. She radiated such happiness. My eyes welled with tears.

Joe would become her primary person, to have and hold in sickness and in health. I dabbed my face with a tissue and remembered how the school had made us go to separate classrooms on the first day of kindergarten. How Mom had never said a word about us being separated. Instead, she made school sound great with words like "new friends" and "fun learning." But she was wrong. For a long time, I was too sad at being apart from Lou Ann to make new friends.

After the ceremony came a sit-down dinner, too many toasts, and finally the cutting of the cake. My feet hurt. After gathering their presents and heaping them into the trunk, Lou Ann and Joe drove off in his old sedan— not on a honeymoon, but to their one-bedroom rental near the University of Minnesota. Joe had to work at his job at the university on the following Monday.

Walking into our bedroom, I kicked off the horrible shoes and pulled down the bridesmaid dress, stepping out of it with care. I hung it up on my side of the closet, even though I knew I would never wear it again. There was a band of bright red skin all around my waist. Slipping into my night-gown, robe, and slippers felt like heaven. As I sat on my bed in my too-quiet bedroom, I wanted some more champagne—something, anything to fill the emptiness inside. Every time I looked at Lou Ann's empty bed my chest hurt. Maybe I could pretend she was away at summer camp being a counselor like she had in other years. Instead, I found an empty cardboard box and began packing.

Two weeks later I was living in an apartment on campus with my new roommates, Karen and Terri. They were also students at the university living away from home for the first time. We talked about everything, but I'd noticed the subject of mothers came up often. Usually I changed the subject or found something else to do, aware of the pressure building inside me. If I talked about my mother, who was dead, or about my sister, who was no longer in my life in the same way, I knew I'd burst.

But I also longed for relief from that pressure. From the agony of phone calls asking to speak to my mom—another reason I was glad to live on campus—and from the conversations that everyone else was part of, except me. It came to a head one afternoon. I walked into the living room where Karen and Terri were chatting on our ratty, plaid couch, a give-away from one of their homes, and I realized they were talking about their families once again.

Karen turned to me, smiling, wanting me to be included. "Linda, does your mother dye her hair?" The warm air in our sunny living room grew heavy with stillness. I watched dust motes in the beam of sunlight, forming the words in my head. Finally, I spoke. "My mother is dead." A profound silence settled over the room. Karen stared at me, then jumped up from the couch. "I forgot about my laundry downstairs. Come with me, Terri?" I put my face in my hands, listening to their footsteps until the door clicked closed.

I'd said "dead" and "mother" together for the first time since Mom died. I waited for the ceiling to fall down, or for my body to explode into thousands of pieces. "My mother is dead," I said again to the empty room. A thick wall inside me broke open, and harsh sobs poured from my throat. I pushed my face into the dusty couch cushions and screamed. The screams sounded like a bulldozer, destroying everything in their path. I wore myself out crying, eyes burning and lungs heaving, but sitting in the empty apartment oppressed me. Taking my keys I locked the apartment and walked the three blocks to the Mississippi River, where I wandered down a footpath until I got to the bank. Sitting on a log, watching the brownish water stream by, I remembered the endless admonishments from my parents to be strong and not cry. I'd heard that message my entire life. "You're such a baby. Nobody likes a whiner. You stop that crying, or I'll give you something to cry about." I'd just broken that rule and it left me buoyant and alive. I stayed on that log, immersed in a quiet peacefulness until the sun began to set and the mosquitoes started to bite.

The next morning when I got up, my roommates had already left for class. Outside my window, I heard the whistle of a chickadee. On my way to my first class, the warm sun was a caress on my skin and the air smelled sweet, carrying notes of the approaching spring.

8

Copper Saucepans and Tarnished Silver

Copper saucepans on the stove sparkled in the bright sun, and the fragrance of cilantro filled Lou Ann's small kitchen. Over a year had passed since her wedding, and I liked this new cozy apartment she'd rented with Joe. It wasn't that far from my apartment, so we saw each other frequently. Tonight, she'd invited me to help her cook for a small dinner party. Cooking with my twin was like a dance without words. I could tell from a subtle shift in her posture, or how she looked at the ingredients what she'd do next. She put the recipe between us on the counter and with barely a word, we'd put together a fabulous meal.

We talked while she minced garlic and I sliced onions. I realized that marriage hadn't changed my sister all that much, except for a level of tension in her that grew in tiny increments, especially when I was at their house. I knew that Joe didn't like me. He'd acted friendly while they were dating, but as time passed he'd become more and more antagonistic. It was easier to spend time with Lou Ann on nights when Joe was gone, like tonight, but the whole setup rubbed me the wrong way.

"Joe doesn't like me, does he?"

My sister stopped chopping broccoli and looked at me. "He's an only child, so he doesn't get twins."

"Have you tried explaining how it is between us?" But I knew it was more than that. There was actual animosity between us, as if he hated me for no reason I could tell—unless Lou Ann had told him about my newfound attraction to women.

"I tried." She sighed. "He's changed." Her shoulders sagged as she resumed chopping vegetables. "I know," she said, a moment later. "Let's have some wine." She pulled a bottle out of the fridge and poured us each a glass. "It'll make cooking more fun," she said, turning up the radio.

Taking a sip of wine, I remembered the house party Dad had for his singles group about a year after Mom's death. Crème de menthe, crème de cacao, and Kahlúa all tasted wonderful mixed with milk over ice. Dad was so busy with his friends that he never noticed us going back to the table again and again for refills. Later, Lou Ann vomited all over the bathroom floor, yelling, "Whoosh, I'm a fountain!" I stopped drinking long before she did that night.

In Lou Ann's small dining room, the food was on the table, and her three work friends gathered around. "Let's eat," Lou Ann said as she filled her glass again, "and please have more wine." That made four glasses she'd drunk since I'd arrived to help with dinner; I was still on my first. Bowls of steaming jasmine rice and chicken stir-fry circulated as the conversation turned to classroom and administration problems they shared at the school where they all worked part-time. Everyone joked, but when Lou Ann talked, they listened. I noticed how much they admired her, and I felt proud. The conversation became more and more animated as the evening continued. Finally, plates were pushed aside and Lou Ann served us bowls of lemon sorbet.

"Anyone want more?" Lou Ann asked. Her words were slightly slurred and as she poured, a little wine spilled on the tablecloth. I felt a warm flush rise up on my neck. Was Lou Ann drinking because she was unhappy with Joe or still upset over Mom's death?

"Lou Ann, that was a delicious dinner, but I've got to get home," the youngest teacher said. She stood up, and the others followed her.

"I'll help with dishes," I said after everyone left.

"That would be great. I just need to sit here for one minute."

I immersed my hands in the warm soapy water and began washing plates and putting them in the second sink to be rinsed. The sound of the door opening startled me. Joe was home.

"Oh, it's you," he said, his mouth turned down in disgust. "I should have known she was up to something. Friends from work, like hell." He threw his car keys on the kitchen counter and stomped past me into the living room over to Lou Ann, who was sleeping on the couch.

"Joe, stop it." I dried my hands and followed him. "Her work friends just left."

"And look here, she's passed out again." He put his face close to her ear. "Wake up, Lou Ann!"

She startled.

"Joe!" I said. "Stop!"

His face contorted with rage. "She's *my* wife."

"Go home, sis." Lou Ann said, her eyes fluttering open. "Just leave."

I walked home through the cold winter air to my apartment, feeling an ache in my heart about Lou Ann. I couldn't believe what I'd just seen. Within a year, the sparkling promise of their wedding vows had tarnished, just like the silver tea service Lou Ann inherited from Mom. Lou Ann had always been the golden one, the strong one, the twin who protected us and even stood up to Mom.

Every time I mentioned my concerns, Lou Ann defended Joe. And even though she reassured me many times over the next few weeks that she and Joe were good, I still worried. I felt I should have paid more attention at the beginning of their relationship, or spoken up sooner.

I hoped that Diane, an astrologer I'd met through friends, would have answers. For the last two weeks everyone I knew had been buzzing about how "right on" she was. Diane had been trained by her aunt, a well-known local psychic. I made an appointment for the following Friday. Maybe she'd help me understand what was happening with Lou Ann and what, if anything, I could do to help.

9

A Dark Shadow

Walking across campus for my meeting with Diane, I wasn't sure if my heart was pounding from fear or my fast-paced walk. I'd been interested in the stars even before the first time Lou Ann and I sat on the warm sand by Devil's Lake and looked up at the constellations. But astrology was different, exciting, new.

I recognized Diane immediately—she was short with curly auburn hair, and her nose and cheeks were covered with freckles. We said hello, then found a quiet spot to sit on the warm steps outside of Coffman, the student union. Diane lifted a large, green vinyl bag off her shoulder and pulled out a thick, hardcover book with "Ephemeris 1900–2000" embossed in gold on the front. The way the gold lit up in the sunlight made me think something very special was about to happen.

"What's that?" I asked.

"This lists the positions of the planets every day. It's a major tool of the astrologer's trade." She started to page through it. "When's your birthday?"

"September 1, 1948."

The pages were full of numbers and odd symbols set in long, neat rows. Somehow they were mysterious but familiar at the same time. The book smelled faintly of spicy incense. I wanted to touch the page, make contact with those symbols. Even though the darkness that weighed on me after Mom died had lifted, I still felt a hollow space inside my chest. That space had grown since witnessing Joe's treatment of Lou Ann.

Diane put an index card under a line of numbers. "You're a Virgo sun with a Leo moon." She said, looking up at me. "That makes you a perfectionist with high standards and a need to be right." She ran her hand through her hair, brushing it behind her ear. "Is that true?"

I thought for a moment about how the smallest details, a hair in the sink or a paper sticking out from a pile, were always getting under my skin. "A perfectionist for sure," I said. "I don't always need to be right. That sounds more like my twin, Lou Ann."

"I didn't know you were a twin." Diane said. "Most of what I say will be true of your sister as well." She continued. "Leo moon people can be very creative, and usually love children. They love being in the spotlight, but not you. You have Pluto right there on your moon." Her voice went soft on the word Pluto. So soft I had to strain to hear her.

"What's Pluto?"

"Pluto represents the dark shadow or underworld, and moon is mother." She paused. "It says something difficult happened to you about age eighteen."

My arms were suddenly very cold despite the warm, bright sunlight, and I hugged myself. How could she possibly know that Mom had died and when? We'd just been introduced.

"What is it, Linda?"

"Our mom died when we were seventeen." My heart still hammered as I said those words, even three years later. "How could you know that?"

What I didn't say, and wished I could, was that Mom was a dark shadow while she was alive. I was becoming a different person without her constant control and criticism—a lighter, happier version of myself.

"I'm so sorry." Diane's face flushed. She looked down at the book again. "I'm just interpreting the planets." She paused. "Do you want to keep going?"

"Yeah, go ahead."

I learned from Diane that I was a people person, that in a couple years I would have troubles in love, which sounded better than no love at all, and that my profession would involve communication. We spent about an hour together; then I thanked her and left.

The meeting had only given me more questions, not answers. I was intrigued with the Ephemeris. I could still see those amazing pages with all their secrets, and I wanted to know more. Diane's predictions seemed as if they could be true for lots of people, but the dark shadow with the mother and the difficult period around age eighteen rattled around in my head for days. How could some distant planets associated with my birthday reveal such a deep truth? It was as if she'd been inside my head, understanding things about my life that even I didn't know.

That week and the next, I saw little of Lou Ann. My sister and I talked when we could, mostly at breaks between classes but rarely when she was home. I could tell her situation was getting worse, and I wanted so badly to tell her about the meeting with Diane, ask her help in understanding what I'd learned.

I realized the best way to help Lou Ann would be to study that book, learn as much as I could from it, and see if there were ways to improve our lives—both our lives. But as long as she was married to Joe, I didn't hold out much hope.

10

Glittering Galaxies

The silver light of the full moon streamed through my thin curtains onto the bed, waking me from a deep sleep. I pulled on fleece-lined slippers and grabbed my robe off the nearby chair. *The A to Z Horoscope Delineator* was open to the page I'd been reading before I went to bed. Four months had passed since my meeting with Diane, and I'd become obsessed with astrology.

I walked to my desk and sat down to study. Reading astrology books sometimes made the top of my scalp tingle, and often I had the distinct impression of remembering something I already knew. Finally, I'd found something that made sense, and it began to fill the emptiness inside me. I moved the *A to Z* and opened C. E. O. Carter's book to read about Saturn in conjunction to the moon, something I'd seen in my birth chart. I started on page sixty-nine.

"The temperament is hard, self-seeking and critical with few good words for anyone, though such praise as they may not grudge is usually well bestowed, and criticism is not so actuated by envy or a carping spirit, as it is the outcome of an almost inordinate craving for perfection." This sounded so much like Mom; she must have it in her chart too, I thought. Maybe her perfectionism was why she couldn't praise anyone. Was I a hard person? A seeker for perfection? I knew somewhere inside these books I would find answers.

As I often did during these early morning sessions, I drifted off, my head falling to my chest. What followed had never happened before. In a dream I flew effortlessly through outer space, in a vast, star-studded world—a world of darkness where the darkness was infused with light. The light penetrated every cell in my body and mind until I felt completely dissolved and illuminated. Constellations streamed by, and whorl-shaped galaxies glittered in the distance, more majestic and beautiful than anything I'd ever imagined. I floated amidst the rings of Saturn and marveled at their dusty reflective particles; hues of blue and gray caressed my being. A moment later I was orbiting with the seven moons of Jupiter as the gas giant bubbled and sizzled. Its brightness was beyond anything I'd known and it filled me with joy. The entire time a subtle vibrational music filled my ears like harmonics on a guitar after the strings are plucked. Notes rippled and faded slowly, sounding like the aftermath of a ringing gong. An immense sense of perfection, wholeness, and peace filled me.

That dream was more real than anything I'd experienced in my life. When I woke, still at my desk, I grabbed my notebook and pen and wrote it down, my hand flying across the paper. I'd visited deep space and the planets. I met Saturn, face-to-face. I'd experienced firsthand the majesty of the planets I'd been studying; I felt their vibrations, heard their music, and became one with them.

As soon as I was done writing, I opened the curtains to look at the sky where a white wonderland of fresh snow greeted me. The moon was gone, and the sky was just starting to brighten. Time for a cup of coffee and a shower. Maybe the hot water would help the ache in my neck. Pain was a small price to pay for space travel, I thought as I filled the coffee pot with grounds and then water. I had to tell someone the dream. I hoped I could reach Lou Ann after my shower.

"After Saturn, I visited Jupiter, the gas giant," I told her. The sun filled my small apartment kitchen with a special light that glimmered off the snow-laden branches.

"You had what they call a lucid dream. I learned about it in psychology class." My sister blew on her coffee, then sipped and swallowed. "It's an alternate state of consciousness."

I poured myself another cup. "I think it's a sign I'm meant to be an astrologer."

Lou Ann was silent for a beat, then another. "How will you ever make a living doing something like that?"

THE WIND BIT through my wool winter coat as I pulled my scarf up to cover part of my face. The bus that would take me to art history class at the University of Minnesota was running late. "Damn cold," an older man in a big fur hat muttered as we climbed the metal steps onto the warm bus.

"Damn Lou Ann," I thought as I settled into my seat. Why couldn't she get excited for me? Astrologers must be able to make a living, and so what if I was poor? I didn't have money now and managed anyway. I leaned my head against the window and watched my breath make a big foggy circle, realizing a terrible truth about my sister.

Lou Ann was turning into Mom.

11

Altered Consciousness

arly morning fog spread over black and green fields of soybeans as we
roared along the road. I held tight to Steven's back, trying to get comfortable on the hard motorcycle seat. He and I shared many classes and had struck up a close friendship. Some mutual friends had invited us to an early morning party at an old farmhouse deep in the country where we were going to drop LSD. I could feel centuries of familial disapproval rise up, even as I imagined taking drugs.

It was the late 1960s, and everyone wanted to raise their consciousness and explore new frontiers. A few friends had raved about their amazing experiences with psychedelics, and I wanted one of my own, particularly after flying through space with the planets in my dream. I was torn, though: we had been raised to follow society's rules, no questions asked. But Mom had been gone well over three years, and although her death had shocked and hurt me, it had also opened me to new freedoms. Not allowed an adolescence while she lived, I'd started to question everything she'd taught me.

Eight college-aged friends of friends sat around the farmhouse's big wooden table as Steven's friend passed out small, oval throat lozenges. The strong licorice flavor was pleasant as I let it dissolve on my tongue. They told us the drug took an hour to take effect, so I decided to take a walk outside.

Nature always soothed me; it was where I found myself most peaceful and alive. In the years after we left high school, Lou Ann and I had hiked, backpacked, and canoed with a passion.

I found a small hill and climbed up to a clearing. Birds trilled their morning songs around me; above me were only trees and sky. I breathed in the clean country air and felt as if I'd left my concerns about money, college, and work back in town. The night before, as had become my new habit, I'd looked at the ephemeris: the planets were aligned in favorable positions to my chart. Today would only bring me a positive experience; I knew it in my bones.

Minutes passed. Then the world crystallized into high resolution. The dappled movement of sun and shade on birch trees created elaborate, alluring, and magical visual patterns. A distant creek changed from a murmur to an orchestra. The very ground I sat on hummed with energy as I took a deep breath and my consciousness lifted above my body. Suddenly I was viewing everything from above—the expanse of farmland that stretched for miles, the trees moving in the wind, the small figure that was me sitting on the hilltop. I was part of every living thing, enveloped in an energy of oneness.

I closed my eyes and felt the grass and earth below me. As the warmth of the sun caressed my skin, I melted into my surroundings. I dissolved into the water in the creek moving swiftly over rocks, pushing against the banks and flowing downstream. Then I was the wind ruffling the leaves on the trees at the same time as I was the leaves feeling moved by the breeze. Joy and awe filled me as I laughed out loud, still seeing myself from above, a small young woman in the middle of nowhere, connected to everything.

Sometime later, as the sun dipped behind the trees, I walked back to the farmhouse. My connection with the world had left me changed, more open and awake. I heard music streaming out the screen windows. Steven and his friends sat on the mismatched couches, jamming with guitars, bongos, and tambourines. I found a chair and leaned back, letting the sound fill me.

Then another strange thing happened: the wall next to me slowly dissolved, becoming transparent. The outer form of the wall remained, but I could see into a bedroom that contained a messy bed, a dark brown dresser, and clothes on the floor. Part of me knew that seeing through walls was impossible, so I left my chair and walked down the hall to check it out. The room was exactly as I'd seen it. Standing in the doorway, I let my eyes go soft, and the wall dissolved again: there were the musicians on their couches as if we were in the same room. In that moment, I understood what Albert Einstein meant when he wrote that reality is an illusion.

We crashed at the farmhouse that night, and I awoke refreshed and in a state of great excitement. The world I had known and my understanding of reality had shattered. In its place was another kind of knowing. All life was interconnected, and humans were capable of much more than we imagined. If not for our everyday limited consciousness, we would all live inside the divine.

I didn't care that it had been a drug that gave me this glimpse of another reality. LSD had shown me that Mom was wrong. I was and always had been whole, beautiful, and connected to something universal, transcendent, and perfect. When I called to tell Lou Ann about my experience, I could hear disapproval in her voice, an echo of how I imagined Mom might react. In her life with Joe there was no place for psychedelics, although the supply of wine seemed endless.

A week later when we met for lunch, though, she asked me to describe my experience on the hilltop for a second time. She asked so many questions that, in spite of the judgment in her voice, I knew she wanted to be on that hill with me. Like me, she was seeking something beyond what we all knew.

12

A Strong Root Chakra

I tried to keep Lou Ann's disapproval from tarnishing our conversations, but it kept creeping in. Many months passed when I braced for criticism, waiting for her to present doubt and make me feel bad about my growing enthusiasm for altered states of consciousness and astrology. Even when we didn't agree, a lingering image from the planet dream or a memory of the leaves on the countryside hill would remind me that I had changed. Then Lou Ann began softening bit by bit over time, being less harsh, agreeing with me a bit more. The biggest change came two years later, when she finally said she was leaving Joe and filed for divorce. Once her divorce became final, instead of criticizing my new passions, Lou Ann began to share her own. My sense of her longing to be on that hill with me was right.

"My reading with Roberta Miller was totally amazing," she told me when we got together one afternoon. A smile lit her face. I loved seeing my sister so excited about life again, just like when we were kids. Her divorce had been final for two months, but she'd been living with friends for six. Along with leaving Joe she'd decided to change careers. I was thrilled when studying gestalt therapy opened her to astrology, psychics, and even Reiki healing. College was behind us and I was living alone, making money doing astrology readings and cleaning houses part-time. And, even better, Lou Ann and I were back on our shared path. When Lou Ann learned that Roberta, a well-known psychic from Esalen Institute, was coming to town, we'd signed up for her weekend workshop on centering, and Lou Ann booked an individual session.

"Promise you'll book an appointment soon," she said. "Her schedule is almost full."

We sipped iced tea at the coffeehouse around the corner from Roberta's temporary office as Lou Ann handed me a slip of paper. "Here's her number."

I tucked it into my jeans pocket. "I'll call right away."

I trusted Roberta because of something that happened at the weekend workshop. During a guided imagery, when we focused on our throat chakras I felt something cut off my air supply, and I began to choke. Panicked, I opened my eyes to see Roberta holding her hands close to my neck. The suffocation immediately diffused.

"Breathe into the sensation," she said, her hands radiating warmth. I took a breath and closed my eyes again. "Good. Now relax your diaphragm."

As I inhaled, a white light burst from behind my eyes and pushed out the top of my head. I was floating high above a grassy meadow. Below, a gray-haired woman's body hung from a tree, a noose around her neck. I knew she was me. I felt the same feelings that had come up during my planet dream and my experience with LSD; my consciousness was suffused with light and joy. I wanted to stay there forever.

"You remembered a past life," Roberta said softly as I felt my consciousness slide back into my body. "It's very common to remember the final moments."

Although I didn't know it then, that would become the first of three times I would remember a past life. Each of those memories would leave me feeling deeply changed.

In the coffeeshop, Lou Ann cleared her throat. "Can I tell you about my reading?"

"Tell me everything." I said, sipping my tea.

"She talked about a block in my throat chakra and how that meant it was hard to speak my truth." Lou Ann played absently with a ring of moisture on the table left by her glass. "I think she's right about that."

"Yeah, we were trained to be seen and not heard." I watched a server bring two hot chocolates tall with whipped cream to a table where a couple sat holding hands and laughing.

"Then she worked on opening a blockage in my heart chakra, saying something about a loss in my life that had caused me to close off that energy." A shadow moved across her eyes, turning them from blue to gray as she studied the table again.

I'd never told Lou Ann about my tearful breakdown the day I admitted to my roommates and myself that Mom was dead. I wondered if my sister had experienced anything similar, if she had ever really grieved our dead mother.

"But my favorite part," she said, looking up and smiling, "was about my center, or root chakra. She saw a small red sphere resting at the base of my spine." Her smile grew wider. "She said it was solid and strong, one of the best she'd seen." The entire weekend workshop had been about developing a center, or home base, and the great value in having one. Not only would a center add to a person's vitality, but it would free them from needing outside approval, something that I sought too often.

I tried imagining a small red sphere at the base of my spine and couldn't. Even if I had a center waiting to be discovered, it was just like Lou Ann to find out first.

"What does it mean?" I set my empty glass on the table, preparing myself. Once again, my sister had risen higher than I ever could. Everything she touched turned to gold.

"My survival energy is so strong that I'm able to overcome most obstacles."

"Wow." I didn't know what else to say. "Can you feel it?"

"I feel it all the time."

I couldn't wait to call Roberta when I got home. I wanted to have a strong center like Lou Ann.

ROBERTA TOOK A deep breath, and another. I shifted on the cushion, trying to relax.

"Well," she said after a moment, "there's a lot of muddy energy around your heart and throat chakra." I waited. "It suggests that you bear emotional wounds that make it hard to speak up." OK, I could buy that. I often held myself back, and she'd said something very similar to Lou Ann. "Give me a moment to work with those energies."

I closed my eyes and moved my awareness to my heart chakra, hoping for another experience similar to the past life memory, but I only felt blank.

"That's better," she said, after a short minute passed. "Your third eye is remarkably open, and I imagine you get overwhelmed at times by other people's energies."

"Yes, when I give astrology readings."

"I can't work on that chakra, it's too sensitive, but I recommend you use the clearing meditation I taught you."

I knew the meditation would help, and I was glad to hear about my third eye, but it was time to move on to what was really important. What Lou Ann had learned. "Can you tell me about my root chakra?"

Roberta closed her eyes again. A moment passed. Then another. Finally she opened her eyes again. "I can't really speak to that. I'm sorry." Her voice was soft, almost apologetic.

I felt a trickle of sweat run down the back of my neck. "You said Lou Ann had one of the best."

"There's no energy in your root chakra at all, Linda." She looked at me sadly. "I'm afraid you don't have a center."

Heat rushed over my body, and for a moment I thought I was going to faint. I looked around, trying to figure out what to do. I knew I couldn't stay with Roberta in that room, not a moment longer with what she'd just said. How could I have felt the connectedness of the universe and not have a center? I gathered myself and stood up, pulling fifty dollars from my wallet. I threw the money on the desk. "I have to go," I said. And I did, without a backward glance.

I could hear Roberta's voice behind me as I ran down the steps to my car. "Linda, come back," she called, but I kept on going.

I had no center. Not even a weak one. Something deep inside deflated in those few moments, and it seemed as though it would take time to get it back. Since Mom died, I thought I'd overcome so many negative messages, but apparently not enough. On top of that, I worried about one thing: How would I tell Lou Ann? She was so proud of her center, one of the best Roberta had ever seen. Lou Ann was always best. No wonder Mom favored her. I should know better than to even try.

13

Reiki Healing

Not having a center bothered me for weeks. I couldn't tell Lou Ann, I decided, so I kept our phone conversations brief. I knew if I mentioned it, she'd say something compassionate that would make me feel worse. She never *tried* to make me feel worse; I never questioned her love. But somehow it always happened that I felt slightly below her. During those same weeks, it seemed every time I went out to the post office or grocery store, I was mistaken for Lou Ann. So when I needed a haircut, instead of going to the hairdresser we both used, I went to a new salon. I worked with the stylist to create a new look, and then I traded in my contact lessons for glasses. Eagerly, I waited for friends and coworkers to notice, but nothing changed.

I loved being a twin, but there were times when I wondered why things came easier to Lou Ann. I decided I had to find out why. The first step would be learning how to grow a center. It must be possible to develop one, I thought, so when I ran into Diane at a social event, I took her aside and quietly asked her for recommendations. She gave me the name of a Reiki healer she trusted. I set up an appointment with Doris for the end of the month.

I didn't know much about Reiki. It was well-respected in the new age circles I traveled in as an astrologer, but I didn't expect the middle-aged woman with a wide, pleasant face and salt-and-pepper hair who answered the door of her home in south Minneapolis. She looked so ordinary, so unhealer-like. But I trusted Diane and Diane liked Doris, so I put my jacket and purse on a coat rack and followed her to a small room with a chair and a massage table.

"There's no need to take off your clothes for Reiki, but I suggest you take off your watch and shoes. I have a blanket, so just tell me if you get cold."

Doris turned on some flute music, dimmed the lights, and stood beside me. "I want you to take five long, deep breaths, breathing in through your nose and out through your mouth. I'll hold my hands above your body and send healing energy wherever I sense you need it." She paused. "Let's begin."

Detaching from the chatter of my mind like Roberta taught us, I breathed and waited. When I cracked my eyes open, I could see Doris moving her hands in figure-eight patterns above my chest. I closed my eyes again. Moments passed. Suddenly, I felt a searing pain in both of my wrists. My arms began to throb. I stifled a moan.

"Tell me what you see." Doris's voice was calm and reassuring.

I was outside my body, looking down as the spasms subsided. "Blood is gushing from the stumps at my wrists." I felt like I was in a dream or watching a play. "Someone cut off both hands. They said I'd broken the law."

Doris placed warm gentle hands on top of mine. "In a past life you were killed for being a healer," she said, squeezing lightly, "just like me." She removed her hands. "I saw that image hovering above you from the moment you walked in." She paused to let it sink in. "Tell me when you're ready, and I'll continue the treatment."

After the memory diffused, I could feel a subtle warmth following Doris's hands as she moved to my torso and legs. I wondered if any other memories would surface, and one did—a fleeting recollection of Shel forcing his tongue into my mouth many years earlier. I felt heat rush over me again and I managed to push it away. Doris didn't seem to notice. Soon the session ended. When I opened my eyes, the room looked crisp and clear, as if my vision suddenly improved.

Walking to my car, I thought about the session and what Doris told me before I left. She said I needed to take back power I'd given to an abuser. That thought rattled around my head for days until I made a decision and called Lou Ann. Together, over the next weeks we came up with a plan to include Dad and confront Shel at his office.

I HELD LOU Ann's hand as we rode up to the twelfth floor of the downtown Minneapolis office building. In the weeks since my session with Doris, I'd been on a quest to find where Shel worked. It was easy enough to make an appointment with his secretary. Much more difficult was convincing Dad to support me by showing up. "It was eleven years ago, Linda," he said now, leaning against the side of the elevator, his hands jingling change inside his pockets. "Why can't you leave it in the past?"

"I just can't," I said, exiting the elevator and pulling open the heavy glass door. The receptionist took my name, and before I could even sit down, Shel was there. My entire body went into high alert.

"What a pleasant surprise." His voice was smooth as always, but he had changed. His thick brown hair was completely gone on top, and the two front buttons of his dark blue suit strained against his big round belly. Unbuttoning his jacket, he led us to his office and sat behind a large desk.

"How are—"

"This isn't a social visit." I took a deep breath, calling on all my inner resources, and gathered myself. "I recently remembered that you sexually assaulted me." My heart was pounding hard, but I'd practiced this with my therapist. I felt Lou Ann slide closer to me on the couch where we sat.

"You can't seriously—"

"Listen." I stood up and walked toward his desk, placing a hand on the mahogany expanse. "Our mother was dead for one month, and you took advantage of me. You were an adult, and I was seventeen years old." I let the rage I still felt fill my eyes. "I deserve an apology." I said this quite loud, while muttering under my breath, "you worthless piece of shit."

There was a silence. Then Lou Ann stood up and walked to my side. "I've known about it all these years," she said. "Apologize to her. Now."

Shel looked out the window. He shifted around in his chair. An apology squeaked out, a faint "sorry." It was half-hearted at best, but I decided to not push it. I'd said my truth, and that mattered most. Maybe I'd get that center I longed for.

"We're done, then," I spat at him. "Goodbye, Shel." Lou Ann and I headed to the door.

I saw Shel stand up and Dad walk over to him. "I tried stopping her, Shel, I really did," Dad said. "Sorry to bother you like this."

I turned around just as Shel said, "No harm done," and Dad shook his hand.

Trembling with fury, I turned to Lou Ann, "Did you see that?"

She grabbed my hand. "Let's go. Dad has his own car." We ran to the elevator, pushing the button twice, hoping it would hurry, hoping Dad wouldn't get in.

"I hate him."

"Dad or Shel?" Lou Ann asked, pushing the P button for parking.

"Both, but I hate Dad more."

The doors closed, sealing the two of us off from the world.

14

Life's Mysteries

Dad's behavior remained a mystery to me, and a few weeks later, during a car trip to Rocky Mountain National Park in Colorado, I asked Lou Ann why Dad would shake Shel's hand. She shrugged. "Maybe it was his way of saving face?" She kept her eyes focused on the road.

"I embarrassed him?"

She looked over at me. "We did show up unexpectedly." She fiddled with the knob on the radio and then turned it off. "And Dad doesn't like conflict—that's why he tiptoed around Mom."

"He acted like he cared more about Shel's feelings than mine," I said. "I'm still mad."

She reached over and patted my shoulder. "And you have every reason. My guess is there's more to Dad's reaction than we know."

I DIDN'T KNOW what that could be, but I knew astrology. When Lou Ann asked me to do a session for her friend Jan, who was in the midst of a difficult time, I agreed, even though I didn't like doing astrology away from my home office and books. We stopped at her home on the way to the national park.

I sat across from Jan on her living room couch, charts on a coffee table between us. "In six months, you'll be through the worst of the legal issues, and the divorce will most likely be final then." It was a relief to be thinking about Jan's problems, not mine.

She brushed her hair away from her face. "Harry always hated change," she sighed, "but I had no idea he'd be so vindictive when I asked for a divorce."

I studied the chart I'd drawn up, looking over the transiting planets that described what was going on now. "I see how terrified he is of losing you, but he's even more terrified of losing control. After you're legally separated, he may still try to make you pay emotionally."

She sighed again. "His lawyer said he wants to change the custody arrangements. He knows I hate being away from the boys. Is that what you mean?"

Such suffering, I thought. "Get everything in writing, especially about custody. That would be my suggestion."

Jan looked down at her hands. "Did I make a mistake? Putting the boys through this?"

I could tell from the chart that she hadn't, but it was hard to reassure her when she couldn't read the stars herself. I reached over and patted her arm. "From what I see, a cycle's coming that promises you both freedom and a major new beginning. It'll start in about a year. Just hold on till then."

Jan looked relieved. She gave me the first real smile I'd seen in our session and thanked me for her reading. Before we left, I overheard her talking about it with Lou Ann but I couldn't make out what they said. My sister and I got back into the car and drove up the road, heading to the mountains. Time passed. Lou Ann didn't say a word, just stared at the scenery. I turned on some music, only a little disconcerted by her silence. Had Jan said something to her that made her regret asking me to do the session?

We pitched the tent in silence, set up our campsite, and set off for a short hike.

The aspen forest was brilliant in the afternoon sun. The greenish-white bark seemed to glitter in the cool breeze. I shifted the daypack off my shoulders and onto the ground and took a swig from my water bottle. Lou Ann walked ahead, not waiting for me, and perched on a large rock. I closed my water bottle, put my pack on, and hurried to join her.

"Trail mix?" she offered, her first words since we'd left Jan's. She held out the open Ziploc bag. "Better have some before I eat all the M&Ms."

I took the bag and dug out a few of the bright blue, yellow, and red candies, my favorites. I enjoyed the sweetness and almost immediate burst of energy. We munched in silence, sipping our water and drinking in the fresh mountain air. Even though I'd been biking twenty miles a day for the last two weeks to train for our trip, I couldn't keep up with Lou Ann, no matter how much I pushed myself. For a moment I felt the familiar "less than" feeling. I tried to focus instead on the fresh scent of pine and the cooling breeze.

Still, I wondered at her silence, but my twin had often had these periods of internal reflection, quietude that balanced her talkative, energetic personality. I dismissed the idea that I had somehow offended her or Jan, and decided to let everything be. The stillness was soothing me, and we were too close to have any kind of serious rift.

As I hoisted my pack on my shoulders, Lou Ann pointed off trail. "I want to show you something." I followed her to a large patch of ice that had looked like white snow from the trail. A thin layer of blackness covered the top. She squatted in a patch of wet earth next to the ice. "Look at this." Leaning over, I saw a tiny green shoot about a half inch high. All around it, flecks of sunlight reflected from the damp, icy ground. "In a few weeks this will be a lupine or a columbine," my sister said. "I've been up here when the wildflowers were in full bloom." She broke a thin piece of ice off the edge of the patch to reveal a few even smaller shoots hiding underneath. They were a pale, white-green color. "See?" Her smile lit up her entire face.

"That's life force, all right." I stood up as a cloud passed in front of the sun and the air suddenly cooled. *Time to turn back*, I thought.

Hiking back to our campsite, I kept noticing fallen trees in different levels of decay and decomposition. Some still had leaves and needles, although they'd turned brown, while others looked more like bark and wood chips. Because of my sister's comment, her amazement, I saw them differently now. I kept thinking about the types of new life growing underneath, how endings and even death could fertilize new life.

Exactly what I'd been trying to explain to Jan.

The light was fading when we got back to camp. Lou Ann unzipped the tent and passed me two folding camp chairs. "Be right back," she said. I sat in my chair and gratefully unlaced my heavy hiking boots, peeling off the outer layer of socks and slipping my feet into camp shoes. Then I found a match in my pack and started the fire.

"Here you go," Lou Ann said, handing me a wet, brown bottle of beer. It was icy cold, and yeasty bubbles tickled my mouth as I swallowed. "I put them in the stream under some rocks to stay cold. I always have at least two beers after a long hike. Somehow it keeps my muscles from hurting the next day."

After dinner we pulled our camp chairs close to the campfire. Lou Ann took a long stick and pushed a log onto the coals. The flames burned bright. "Jan loved your reading."

I made my voice casual. "Oh? What did she say?"

"She said you knew things about her divorce that she'd never told a soul, not even her closest friend." Lou Ann paused. "My training in psychology gives me techniques and theories to draw on to help people, but it can take years to get to the heart of what's really going on."

I was quiet, waiting. There would be more.

Then she leaned closer, her eyes reflecting the fire, her voice intense and full of wonder, as it had been while viewing the beginnings of those tiny plants in the alpine forest. "But you know things that other people don't. How does that work?"

15

Homecoming

I thought about the tiny green shoots on the way to the Mud Pie restaurant on Lyndale Avenue where I was about to meet Lou Ann a few weeks after our road trip. We both liked the food and cozy atmosphere, and the big wooden booths were private and comfortable. I chose it as the place where I would reveal my news. Not only did I have a center, as confirmed by the confrontation with Shel and the subtle changes I'd felt since, but I was in love. With someone unexpected. I wanted my sister to be the first to know.

Love hadn't been an easy thing in my life. Lou Ann had married Joe while we were in college, but I'd mostly been a serial monogamist, struggling to be intimate, pushing people away while afraid of being left. But now I knew it, clearly. I'd fallen hard for Molly, and the first time we kissed it felt like a homecoming.

Lou Ann waved at me from a booth facing the door. I hugged her extra hard before I sat down. Once the waitress left with our orders, I leaned across the table, my hands palms up. She put her hands on top of mine.

"You know I've been exploring my sexuality."

Lou Ann nodded.

"I'm in love with a woman." I let out the breath I'd been holding, and waited for her response.

She squeezed my hands and sat back. "Just because I was married doesn't mean I think it's weird. I've had feelings of being sexually attracted to women myself."

I felt my shoulders relax. "What a relief. My housemates have been really cold since I told them." Warmth suffused my belly as it always did when I thought of Molly. "I've never felt like this about anyone before."

"Who is she? Where does she work? How did you meet?" She dipped a spoon into the curried lentil soup the waitress had brought.

"I started going to the Lesbian Resource Center a few months ago. The first time, I was so scared I had to walk around the block three times before I went in." I watched the steam rise off my soup as I stirred it, remembering that life-changing evening. "I forced myself to talk with people. Molly runs a feminist discussion group on Wednesday nights. She's a humanities teacher." I took a cautious spoonful; it was deliciously warming on this chilly fall afternoon. "She's smart and kind. Cute, too."

"In graduate school they made us study the standard classification of mental disorders," Lou Ann said. "Homosexuality was considered an illness—can you believe that? One of my fellow colleagues is gay, and she's the best of the bunch."

**

"So it's settled. We'll tell the folks together." Two years had passed since our lunch at Mud Pie, and recently Lou Ann had called to say she'd fallen in love with a woman.

I could hear the smile in her voice through the phone. "I still can't believe you came out first," she laughed. "I've always been the leader."

"Finally, I'm first!" I said. "Aren't women the best kissers?"

"I'm sure Dad will love hearing that." I heard background noises on her end. "Gotta run, but I'll pick you up at ten on Sunday."

As I hung up the phone, I thought about how our roles were changing. Lou Ann had always been the leader, the strong twin, and now I'd come out first, listening to a small voice inside that said I could trust myself. For so many years, I'd felt inadequate, undeserving of love, but studying astrology, being in therapy, and life with Molly were changing that.

DAD'S CONDOMINIUM WAS at the end of a long hall, but today the hall seemed noticeably longer. We sat inside the high-ceilinged kitchen with four glasses of iced tea on the table between us. Dad's new wife, Henrietta, wore nice slacks with a dressy blouse and, as always, her hair was freshly styled. I found her aloof and critical. I shifted in my chair as Lou Ann sat up straighter.

"We have something important to tell you and hope that being honest will bring all of us closer." Lou Ann's voice was calm, but I knew she was nervous. We'd prepared for weeks by imagining possible scenarios and our best responses. Overhead, the ceiling fan clicked as it turned. I stared at the wet ring around my glass on the table, inhaling and focusing on my feet to ground myself.

"You've been asking me for some time who I'm dating," I said, "and when I'm getting married." My feet felt numb, but I forged ahead. "I want you to know I've been a lesbian for the last three years."

"I'm a lesbian, too," Lou Ann said. "I'm involved with a wonderful woman, a lawyer."

"You're telling us you're both gay?" Dad's face turned pale. He looked at Henrietta.

"Yes, we are."

There was a long silence. Neither of them would meet my eyes. Dad took a big gulp of tea, choked on it, and sprayed tea all over the table. Henrietta hurried to grab a towel.

"Sorry about that." He wiped his mouth. "You caught me by surprise."

Henrietta finally spoke. "Have you been to see a doctor?"

"No one is sick, Henrietta." Lou Ann frowned at her. "We both fell in love with someone who happened to be a woman."

"I brought a book for you to read," I said, reaching into my bag. "It should answer your questions." I handed Dad a paperback copy of *Sappho Was a Right-On Woman*. He set it on the counter without a glance.

"But Lou Ann, you were married. How can you be gay?" Dad said.

"I loved Joe, but Sal is a better fit." She moved slightly in her chair to be closer to me.

"You'll have such sad, lonely lives without a husband or children," Henrietta said.

The rest of our visit was short. We drank a little more tea, I watched Dad shove the book to the far end of the table and Henrietta grimace at it, and then my sister and I stood up.

"It's better that you know," I said. "So you can get used to it."

"I think both you girls need to see a doctor," Henrietta said. "This isn't normal."

"I'll never get used to it," my father said. So we left.

We walked outside into the cool fall sunshine and got into Lou Ann's car. "You know how it took us time to get used to being lesbian?" she said. "They'll come around."

16
Astrology Retreat

*C*oming home to Molly was a balm after the rejection I'd felt from my folks. That evening, she was particularly sweet, telling me how she admired my courage at coming out. "My parents don't know," she said, "and I'm not ready to tell them."

I admired Molly too. She often talked about her happiness at work, and although my astrology business was growing, I had to keep my cleaning jobs since I never made quite enough money to pay my bills.

Later that week, my copy of *Dell Horoscope* arrived, featuring an article about a month-long astrology intensive in California led by Zipporah Dobyns, a well-known astrologer. I knew I had to go.

Zip dressed like an old hippie with her multicolored muumuu, but she was far from it. The biography on the back cover of her five published books mentioned she had three PhDs. Zip explained the rhythm of our days: "In the morning you'll study basic astrological principles and theory, the afternoons will be spent applying the theory, and in the evenings you'll study the psychological principles of astrology."

After just a few days, I knew why it was called an intensive. My brain hurt each evening as I tumbled into bed. Over half the students lived near Los Angeles, while the others came from all over the world. The fee included meals, and we all ate family-style in Zip's large dining room. The days ran into weeks as we immersed ourselves in learning and became intimate with each other's birth charts and lives.

Zip and I didn't agree on everything. She insisted that our higher selves picked not only our time, date, and place of birth, but also our birth family. That meant Lou Ann and I had somehow picked Mom. Who would choose someone so cruel for their parent, I'd wondered and even asked, but our teacher never wavered from her point of view.

Finally, it was time for exams. Sleepless that night, I shifted the pillow under my head and worried. What if I didn't pass? Worse, what if I blanked out and embarrassed myself? Maybe I could get on an earlier flight and avoid it entirely. I'd learned so much from being here, and that was why I'd come. Maybe I didn't need to take the exam. First thing in the morning, I decided, I'd call the airline. I knew it was the height of my Saturn Return, a time to internalize my own authority. Leaving would assert my authority, wouldn't it? Or was I running away? Only that morning, Zip had commented about my struggle to trust myself because of how much I was criticized growing up. She mentioned that I avoided conflict, and running was easier than facing failure and derision. I thought about what she said and how even-handed she'd been with all of her students. Zip wouldn't criticize me; she was a good teacher, and not like Mom. I punched the pillow one more time and decided to see it out, even if I failed.

THE NEXT MORNING, I faced Zip over her antique trestle desk. Three charts I'd hand-calculated lay between us. Next to them, her small paperback ephemeris was open to February 1977. Floor-to-ceiling bookcases covered every wall of her library, and a soft filtered light came in through the gauze curtains. I'd been answering questions and interpreting charts for over two hours.

"Well done, Linda," she finally said. Her blue eyes sparkled behind her glasses. "Not only do you understand astrology, but you have excellent communication skills." A warm heat traveled up the back of my neck and through my scalp. I knew it was because of my center; I had one at last, after what seemed like so many years. I reached across the desk to gather my papers, smiling my thanks. "Oh, we're not done." Zip tapped the eraser of her pencil on the desk. "During the role-play, the questions you asked showed me how well you were able to synthesize the chart. Few people in astrology can do that."

More heat rose. I could barely look at her. "Really?"

She stuck out her hand. "You've passed." I took her soft warm hand and held it for a second. "You'll get a certificate in the mail." She paused, knitting her eyebrows. I waited. "I don't say this to very many people, but I hope you become a professional astrologer. You're really talented."

"That's exactly what I want."

She nodded. "In our final time together, I want to hear a thumbnail interpretation of your birth chart. Outline two strengths and two weaknesses."

I took a deep breath and studied my very familiar chart. I started with a formula we used in class. "This chart has many planets in the seventh and eight houses, showing this person is very people-oriented, and focused on one-on-one relationships." I started to relax into the reading.

"Stop," she said. "Talk about your chart in the first person."

"OK." I swallowed, started again. "I'm a real people person. I love working with people, finding out who they are and what makes them tick. I think that's one of my gifts. But I don't always trust what I know, and I lose confidence and my sense of self."

Zip leaned forward in her chair. "I agree. What can you do to stay grounded in yourself?"

"Keep studying astrology. What else?"

"Go on." Her smile put me at ease.

"The other part of my chart is both difficult and very rich. I have Pluto conjunct the moon, so my natural inclination is to suppress and bury my emotions. That's how I survived growing up. Over time I've learned to face my feelings and accept them. My empathy for myself and my clients has grown."

"We discussed the importance of this during class. Your buried feelings can come out as projections onto your clients, and that will impede your success." She leaned back away from the desk. "Can you find ways to continue your healing?"

Zip's belief in me was stunning. I loved astrology, but this was the first time someone I admired had praised me. I picked up the pencil and rolled it between my fingers, thinking carefully before I answered, because I knew it would matter. A lot. I remembered the therapist who had helped me some years after Mom died, when Lou Ann was in her abusive marriage and when I felt at such loose ends in my life. Zip was telling me I had to heal myself first, before I could help others.

"I worked with a therapist some years ago," I said slowly, "and I could see her again."

17
The Big Fight

Seeing a therapist again wasn't easy. I'd been home for two weeks before I went through my files to find her number. I didn't talk to Lou Ann about it at first, because revisiting all the painful details about our childhood was almost too much to bear. But Zip had been right: there was a lot more to heal in myself. And besides, Lou Ann was busy with her life, her new relationship, the new master's program she'd enrolled in, and her new job at a therapy clinic that had just opened.

Somehow my therapist and I got on the subject of Mom's temper.

"You said things would fly around the room when your mom got mad," the therapist repeated. "What do you think made them fly?"

My face got hot as I remembered Mom yelling at me, sometimes over something small like a scuff on her clean kitchen floor or hairs left in the bathroom sink. The louder she yelled, the more things flew, like kitchen utensils or balled-up papers, but I'd never thought about who threw them.

"She must have thrown them," I said, prickles of sweat gathering in my armpits.

She waited a moment, looking at me. "You're right. And how did that make you feel?"

"Terrified. Ashamed. Alone." I'd been in therapy long enough to know how to name my feelings.

The therapist leaned forward in her chair, her voice gentle, and said, "Take your time and just stay with those feelings." My breath came in gasps, and I began to tremble. "What do you want to say to your mother?" she asked.

"I didn't do anything wrong, Mom. Stop being so mad. You scare me." I sobbed, holding both hands over my face. The feelings washed through me, leaving me drained.

We sat for a moment while I blew my nose and wiped my face.

"Where was your twin when this happened?"

"She tried to stop Mom, but then she'd come down harder on us."

"That's called physical and emotional abuse, Linda," she said. "You didn't deserve any of that."

THREE DAYS LATER Lou Ann and I were walking around Lake of the Isles on a sunny spring morning. All the crab apple trees were in full bloom, and we periodically stopped our fast-paced walk to comment about the various shades of white, the soft and bright pinks, and the sweet smells. I'd been wanting to tell Lou Ann about what I discovered in therapy, but had no idea where to start, so when we got beyond the row of trees, I just blurted it out. "My therapist thinks Mom was physically and emotionally abusive."

Lou Ann stopped walking and turned to face me. "She had a bad temper, and she hit us; all parents spanked their kids back then, but we weren't abused." She shook her head. "In my MA program we learned about alcoholism and drug abuse in families. Now those kids are abused."

"I'm not talking spankings," I said. "It was her rage, the hitting, throwing things, the shaming us; that makes it abuse." I could hear my voice getting louder, so I lowered it as a couple walking a dog went by. Ever since Lou Ann had started the master's program, she acted superior.

She put her hand on my shoulder. "We always had clean clothes, home-cooked meals, toys, and help with homework. Mom was strict, but we learned good life lessons. These kids with drug-addicted parents can go days without a meal; the eight-year-olds have to find something to feed the babies."

I clenched my fists and barreled on. "You stick up for her because you were always her favorite."

Lou Ann shouted, "Stop saying that! She treated us the same."

Here we were again, but I knew I was right. Who cared about other families? Why did studying psychology give her more excuses for Mom? I hated the sweet smell of the crab apple blossoms on the breeze. Why couldn't Lou

Ann agree with me when she knew I needed her support? There were times during our adolescence when she tried to intervene. I walked away and she followed. I turned to face her.

"Remember in sixth grade we were clothes shopping and she told us you'd always look better in clothes because you were taller? How lucky you were that you didn't need glasses because boys don't like girls who wear glasses? How I walked like a penguin and you didn't? That was favoritism," I relaxed my hands, "and mean." Mom's words still hurt me.

"Mom was blunt, but it didn't mean anything." Lou Ann shrugged and walked faster, moving away from me. I let her get ahead, and stopped, listening to my beating heart, my rapid breath. No one could get me mad like Lou Ann, and I couldn't believe her obliviousness on this subject.

I caught up to her. "Maybe not to you."

She grabbed my hand. "C'mon, I don't want to fight with you," she said. "It's such a beautiful day."

I squeezed her hand and let it go. I knew I wouldn't win this argument. Just then a cyclist appeared out of nowhere, and as I jumped off the path I lost my footing on the uneven ground.

"You okay?" Lou Ann asked, reaching out to steady me.

WORK WAS A great distraction from our fight because I was busy, too, handling the new flood of interest in my astrology business.

Molly offered to pay rent for a month or two while I focused on it, even proposed I rent office space, but both ideas made me uneasy. Too many couples broke up over money. So I decided to keep the business at home for a little longer, doing my readings in our dining room while Molly was at work, and juggling my second job cleaning houses.

Six weeks later, the phone woke me from a deep sleep. I left a slumbering Molly and went into the kitchen to answer it.

"I have to ask you something." It was a woman's voice, faintly familiar.

"Who is this?"

"Amy. You did a reading for me last week."

I couldn't believe it. "I'm not working now," I said. "Call during office hours." I slammed the phone into the cradle, the sour taste of adrenaline in my mouth as I stumbled back to bed. Molly was right. It was time to find an office.

Not far from my apartment was a suite of three bright, newly painted offices on the second floor of the Desnick Drugs building. Two massage therapist friends were also ready to move their businesses out of their homes. Last week I'd looked at my chart and Jupiter, the planet of opportunity, was about to enter my fourth house of home and property. I needed to take action right away.

After we signed our names to the year-long contract, and wrote out checks for the first and last months' rent, I chose the center office as mine. I let myself stand right in the middle of the room, admiring the beautiful hardwood trim around the doors and windows, visualizing where my bookshelves and my small wooden desk would go, and where I'd place the consultation chairs. No longer would clients wake me up at home; I'd be official, with my own space. Just as Zip had wanted. Just as I wanted.

The office became everything I'd hoped for: a great place to work that was easy for clients to find, and peaceful. The massage therapists and I chatted when we weren't working, and we grew closer. Every month the extra clients I needed to pay my share of rent seemed to materialize, so I never had to lean on Molly financially. We all agreed to sign on for another year.

✷✷

Damn that phone, I thought as I stumbled out of bed. I'd gone to great pains to make sure everyone had the new office number. Padding barefoot to the kitchen, I picked up the phone.

No moon tonight outside my window, only clouds whisking across a black sky. It was spring again, and we were in the dark moon, or balsamic moon, phase. Zip had explained that the word *balsamico* came from Latin and translated to "restorative" or "curative." *Nothing restorative about the phone ringing in the middle of the night,* I thought as I said hello.

"It's Laura," the voice said. "You did my chart last month." I almost stopped her right there, but an urgency in her voice made me wait. "I thought you'd want to know your office building is on fire."

I jolted completely awake. "I was there this afternoon and everything was fine."

"I was biking home from a dance performance and saw a big blaze. When I got closer, I realized it was your building. The fire department just got it under control."

I thought of all my files burning to ashes. I would have to start over. It would mean hours of calculations for each client.

"Don't worry about your files," Laura said, as if hearing my thoughts. "I told the head firefighter that you're a writer and your life's work was in the file cabinet. I'm standing by it right now."

Relief flooded my body. As I looked outside, the wind blew away the clouds, and for a moment the sky was clear.

The file cabinet would make our entire apartment smell like smoke, but the actual files were fine. A cab driver had navigated through the congested streets that night and helped me carry the heavy file cabinet up the flight of stairs. I promised Laura a free reading and gave the cab driver a big tip.

**

"How'd the fire start?" Lou Ann asked as I climbed in the van she'd borrowed. When I called her, even though the fight was still fresh, she'd immediately volunteered to help me salvage the rest of my office.

"They suspect arson. Someone had a vendetta against the owner of the drug store." I grabbed the armrest as Lou Ann turned around a corner a little too fast. The half dozen cardboard boxes slid around on the metal floor in back.

"That sucks," she said. "You liked it there."

Leaving the flashers on, we headed down the sidewalk. The outside door looked fine, but with each step toward my second story office it became harder to breathe through the strong smell of smoke. Lou Ann pulled a bandanna out of her pocket and covered her nose, making me wish I'd thought to bring one. At the top of the stairs, patterns on the blackened walls showed rolling waves of flames. The plaster ceiling hung down in big chunks. Everywhere, glass crunched under our feet. "Shit. It's bad in here," Lou Ann said as she took my arm to lead me around a pile of debris.

"Ephemeris and table of houses first." These two books were essential to my work. I couldn't construct charts without them. But soot and ash covered everything. I took off my old cotton work shirt and used it to wipe ash off my desk. The two books were right where I'd left them, damp and singed but not burned. We managed to salvage a few more books, but my bookcase, desk, and consulting chairs were beyond repair.

A week later, during a bus ride, I saw the building being torn down. It seemed the good fortune of Jupiter was enough to save my files and books, but not anything else. I tried to be grateful to still have my work, to be able to earn a living, but the fire had shaken me deeply.

18

Things Break Down

After the fire, Molly and I began to fight. I was disturbed by the setback—irritable and short-tempered—and my attempts at working from home backfired fast. Molly had gotten used to me having an office, not cluttering up our shared space with my books and papers. After one particularly terrible fight, I stormed out of the apartment and made my way to Sunsight Books. Nothing was working, my relationship was on the rocks, and I had no idea what to do next. Even studying my beloved ephemeris didn't help.

Sunsight was one of the first new-age bookstores in the Twin Cities, a home for many of us in alternative healing practices. I knew the owner, Marlene, a gifted tarot card reader. I smiled at her when I walked in and headed for the astrology section to look at books. She followed me.

"It's so funny you came in today. I was just thinking of you," she said. "We just finished an expansion, adding an office and classroom space, and we need an in-house astrologer. Someone to teach astrology classes as well. Can we talk about it?"

Dazed, I nodded. Marlene motioned me to follow her up the stairs to the new office. The office was small, barely big enough for the new furniture I needed, and the one small window let in only hazy light. I thought of Molly's angry eyes and the cramped work space waiting at home. I had to get my business out of the house.

"I'm interested. Tell me what you're thinking," I said to Marlene.

**

"You must be the new astrologer," said a young woman with curly black hair and freckles who stuck her head in the door as I unpacked. I'd found great replacement furniture at a nearby thrift store. "I'm Lisa, a psychic." I nodded and beckoned her inside. "Nice moon-sign calendar. I have the same one." We smiled at each other. "I have a feeling this place will be good for you," she said on her way out the door.

Lisa was right. The bookstore brought me new clients and astrology students, and within months I had doubled my workload. Dealing with more clients set off an old familiar challenge. If someone came to see me complaining of back pain, my back would begin to ache. If they had chronic headaches, my head would hurt. My usual clearing and cleansing techniques weren't working.

After a day of five back-to-back sessions, as I headed down to the store on my way home, Lisa waved at me from a bookcase by the front window. "Long day?" she asked.

My body ached with fatigue. "I'm exhausted."

She looked at me very intently. "Your psychic walls are too open, and people's energies are invading you." The smell of spicy incense floated over from behind the counter. I remembered that incense was used to clear energy. I'd burn some tomorrow. "I'll tell you my favorite trick." She leaned in close and lowered her voice. "In between sessions, go to the restroom and run your hands under the coldest water possible. Hold them there as long as you can. Use the water to visualize your entire body being washed clean." She smiled. "Works for me every time. Then mentally I say, 'I release to the universe what is not mine.'"

It became a mantra of sorts, releasing to the universe what was not mine, and slowly I began to find more distance from my client's problems. As I found more distance, it seemed as though more people wanted to see me. Lisa had been right on both counts, and having another person around to talk shop made me enjoy the bookstore that much more.

I was teaching two evening classes at the store, working over forty hours, and through my affiliation with the store, making radio and TV appearances. Lou Ann and I talked on the phone more often than we met in person since she, too, had a full client load plus evening groups at her new clinic. But we still tried to get together regularly—a quick lunch, a cup of coffee, a walk after work. I could feel a change in our relationship, though; something about my own maturing and professional success was helping me feel more independent, not needing her quite as often. Instead, I often found answers by looking in my ephemeris.

"You did great on that TV interview last night." We sat in a crowded coffee shop two blocks from the clinic where Lou Ann worked. "In spite of the interviewer," she shook her head. "What a jerk."

"The fact that Nancy Reagan hired an astrologer is a boon for us all." I sipped my French roast coffee. "Using astrology helps the president's career, and the fact it's front page news helps mine." I didn't really think this was why my practice was booming; Zip had told me it would, and as I kept taking classes and learning from returning clients, I'd grown in confidence.

Lou Ann grinned. "I want you to come to my clinic and do a presentation. Explain how someone in therapy can benefit from an astrology session." I looked at her, remembering the session with Jan, then nodded. We made a date, but a week later Lou Ann called and cancelled. Her clinic was in crisis; the office manager had been stealing the therapists' cash instead of depositing it. She decided to find a new workplace.

A few days later, the morning paper carried the headline "New Age Bookstore Bombed in Possible Hate Crime." Sunsight Books, its big plate glass window blown out, stared at me from the page. Having Nancy Reagan on our side obviously didn't matter. Fire and danger were following me, it seemed, and I remembered how I had almost lost everything in the previous fire. Here I was, professionally forecasting the future, and I couldn't even see my own. I threw my bitter black coffee into the sink as I headed over to see what remained of my office.

Police cars surrounded the block, and yellow tape fluttered in the wind. An officer allowed me to climb the staircase of the business next door. Relief washed through me as I found no damage to my office beyond the pervasive smell of smoke. But the steps going down to the store were charred and burned through in places. Clients would no longer be able to use them to get to my office.

I went back to my office and sat down at my desk, struggling to understand why this happened. The store brought people happiness. We'd created a community for alternative learning, a place for people to find special gifts, crystals, and books and take unique classes. Everyone left enriched by their experiences.

A very pale Marlene stuck her head in the door.

I motioned her in. "Do they have any leads?"

"Not really. A note attached to the bomb said 'evil witches must burn.'" She met my eyes, then looked down. The store carried books on witchcraft, all with a focus on ancient holidays and methods of healing.

"What will you do?"

"We'll have to close for six months." She looked around my untouched office. "You can stay open, you know."

THIS TIME THERE was no eclipse active in my chart, only Uranus, the planet of the sudden and unexpected. Uranus suggested separation, so I decided to move. Within weeks, thanks to my Women in Business group, I found a new location for my practice. But another upheaval in my life proved too much for Molly. Packing boxes were stacked against a wall as I walked in after a long day of moving offices.

"This is how you're leaving me?" I said. "And today?" My body shook with fury.

She shrugged. "I need someone stable, someone who doesn't work every weekend."

I wanted to fight with her, beg her to stay, but I couldn't. In one mighty blow, Uranus upended both work and home. Someone bombed the store because "witches were evil," and Molly didn't love me. What was there to believe in? I felt my center beginning to crumble.

I buried myself in work and found solace in growing my business. My new office had a large classroom space and, frustrated by the teaching schedule at the bookstore, I developed a three-year training program for upcoming astrologers. I wanted to follow in Zip's footsteps and build a legacy of my own. For my first graduating class four years later, I would organize a ceremony, rent folding chairs, have certificates printed, and cater a small feast.

Work success was one thing. Walking into my empty bedroom at the end of a long day was another. I longed to share my happiness with a lover, a partner. Instead I called Lou Ann. She was always happy for me but often cut the call short. She was deeply involved with Elizabeth, a thin, curly-haired outdoorswoman, and they were looking into buying a house.

A FEW MONTHS later, as the smell of fall leaves wafted through open windows, Lou Ann and I spread piles of photos over her round dining room table in her new home to create a collage. For the first time since childhood, we'd decided to commemorate our birthday together with a big party, a celebration for turning forty.

"Look at this one." Lou Ann held out a small black-and-white photo with scalloped edges, "I can't tell us apart, can you?" In the photo, we lay side by side on our stomachs on a 1950s-style flowered bedspread, our heads barely lifted, our hair in identical brown ringlets. "I'd guess we're around three months," she said.

I pawed through the piles, looking for others from that era, when we were so look-alike that nobody knew who was Linda and who was Lou Ann. It was all chronicled in the photos. Our teeth fell out at the same time, our hair grew to the same length, we wore braces at the same time; almost all our physical changes mirrored each other. What distinguished Lou Ann was her height; she was always a bit taller, and in almost every photo she stood slightly in front. I remembered Mom mentioning that our size was the only way they could tell us apart until we started to talk.

Around age three something changed. While Lou Ann looked directly at the camera with a big smile, I looked to the side or down. My smile looked awkward, reluctant even. I remembered Mom telling me I had hernia repair surgery around that time. After the surgery I spiked a high fever and almost died. She took me home from the hospital early and almost sued them for neglect. This event mirrored my birth, when I'd been left in the hospital incubator alone. Later, when I was an adult, during bodywork sessions and in dreams, I'd have brief memories of endless terror and crying for help. I didn't think about it often, but I never forgot it. Instead I gradually internalized a feeling of worthlessness.

I saw it in the photos: my close brush with death, my sense of being different from my sister, even though no one else could tell us apart. But that day, nearing forty, death was far from my thoughts. I could only imagine us forty years in the future smiling into the camera, arm-in-arm, with identical gray hair and matching wrinkles.

19

Chasing the Eclipse

Something about turning forty made me want more adventure in my life. I'd been teaching about eclipses for over ten years when my alumni magazine advertised a university-sponsored trip to La Paz, Mexico, to view the solar eclipse July 11, 1991, with astronomers and professional telescopes, guided sea-life and botany tours, and close to seven minutes of totality. I knew I had to go. I'd never traveled alone or with groups I didn't know and the thought intimidated me, but I'd studied solar eclipses extensively and wanted to experience one. Besides, this eclipse in my chart made a conjunct aspect to Venus, suggesting pleasure, friendship, and even a boost to my work.

My assigned roommate, Cathy, was a few years older than I was, in remission from breast cancer, and one of the most positive people I'd met. After two years of intense treatment she was certain that the disease was gone, and living every day to the fullest was her best defense. Spending time with her at the end of each day reminded me that not everyone who was struck with cancer succumbed to it like Mom did. Because of Cathy's openness I found it easy to confide in her about being an astrologer and the fire at Sunsight books, and we struck up an easy friendship.

On the day of the eclipse we were all bussed to a large schoolyard just outside downtown La Paz, which turned out to be a perfect place to watch. It was empty but for our group of forty, some benches, a few shady trees and a wide, unobstructed view of the sky. As the morning grew hot, an astronomer from the university set up a huge telescope while some of the participants set up their smaller ones. On this trip, for the first time, I met people who chased eclipses all over the globe, hoping to re-experience the magic that came under a dark sun.

If someone had told me then that in 2017 I'd drive ten hours to meet Della in Effingham, Illinois, to view another solar eclipse, I would never have believed them. In spite of spending every day predicting people's future and looking at the ephemeris for myself, I could only fantasize about my own future.

We'd each been given bottled water and a pair of heavy, protective glasses. It didn't take long before the moon's shadow began to cover the sun, and we lined up in groups to look through the different telescopes. The night before, I'd gone onto the roof of our hotel for a viewing of the night sky through the same giant telescope. Venus, Mars, and Jupiter were visible with the naked eye, but through the telescope four of Jupiter's known moons became visible. As I stood with my eye glued to the viewer, I remembered my planet dream from almost twenty years earlier, how Jupiter's surface moved and changed, and I strained to see it clearly. Jupiter's eye was immense and even brighter and more colorful than I'd remembered.

Slowly the sun dimmed, and the light through the leaves formed crescent-shaped shadows; each one looking like a partially eclipsed sun. Within an hour the sky along the horizon turned a sunset shade of pink, and crickets began to chirp. We'd been told to watch the ground to our west for the shadow of the moon as it raced along, preceding the moment of totality. I missed the shadow but felt the strength of a sudden cool wind. All at once the temperature dropped, and day turned to night. Stars shone in the sky as we took turns watching the corona, brilliant fingers of pink and red gas, explode around the black disk of the sun. Something primitive inside me pushed aside all my learning, and I felt a deep irrational fear. I could easily imagine why ancient Indigenous tribes had believed the world was ending when a solar eclipse happened. Collectively we held our breath until a tiny sliver of the sun re-emerged and set things right.

In my astrological study, eclipses brought dramatic changes into the lives of my clients. For large groups of people they were often associated with global disasters: floods, tidal waves, earthquakes, and fires. For individuals they often brought new beginnings in love, jobs, and homes, as well as unexpected illnesses, accidents, losses, and upsets. There was something powerful at work here that went beyond all book learning. Having felt the power of day turn to night, I knew my understanding of eclipses had changed. Life was cyclical and interconnected, vast and powerful, just as I'd experienced years ago sitting on the grassy hillside in the country.

On the plane ride home, I found an article in my astrology magazine on something called a pre-natal eclipse: something that happens while a person is in utero that suggests a difficult time for both the mother and the fetus, along with indicators of the infant's karmic path. After the trip, I pulled out my chart and began searching for more information. I wasn't surprised to learn that my pre-natal eclipse indicated a dark shadowy connection with the mother—the exact thing Diane had mentioned almost twenty years earlier that started me studying astrology. Did my mother intuit she would give birth to twins? That being a parent would be twice as hard as she imagined?

20

Finding Love

I was so tired that Saturday, after seeing seven clients the day before, I almost wrote off my friend Helen's birthday party. She had invited a group of us to get together and go to a water park to celebrate. When Molly and I were together, she had told me so many times that I worked too much. I needed more fun in my life. Now, sitting in Helen's crowded living room, I couldn't keep my eyes off Mindy, the cute, curly haired woman in the black tank top. She was articulate and intelligent, and kept everyone laughing. I was definitely interested.

"It's time to head over to the water park," Helen said. "Leave everything here but your towels and dry clothes." I climbed inside the twelve-seater, and found a spot right next to Mindy. Inside, I'd overheard her talking about backpacking in the Sierra mountains.

"Have you been to the Boundary Waters?" I asked Mindy as I put my plastic bag of dry clothes on the floor next to hers.

"You're the second person to ask me that today." She smiled. "No, but I know how to canoe."

"It's a magical place. I've been going up there for the last twenty years." I spoke loudly over the sound of laughter and women's voices. "The first time we kept our plastic cups tied to the gunwale and just dipped in and drank straight from the lake. You could taste the clean in the water."

Mindy's face lit up as the van pulled away from the curb. "That sounds amazing."

"I'm planning a canoe trip." Helen turned around to face us. "The friends of Helen canoe trip. You're all invited."

Someone hollered from the front. "Count me in."

Mindy looked at me with raised eyebrows. She moved her leg close enough to mine that I felt the warmth radiate off her skin. "I'll go if you go."

My heart did a backflip. "For sure."

Progressed Venus, the planet of love, had been approaching my sun for the last year, and the recent eclipse highlighted it. When I saw this in my clients' charts, many of them fell in love soon after. I had a strong intuition the curly haired woman who made my heart flutter might become someone very special.

✳✳

I was only a little surprised and very pleased when Mindy called a few days later to see if I'd join her the following Saturday for an afternoon walk. The soft summer rain pattered against my raincoat as Mindy and I walked along River Road. I loved that she splashed through puddles with me and agreed a little rain was no reason to change our plans.

"There's something I want you to know, Mindy," I said after a short silence. "I've been obsessed with having children for the last few years." I knew I was taking a risk bringing this up on our second date, but if we were going to continue seeing each other, I had to know where she stood.

She turned to face me, brown eyes glowing. "Me too. I can't believe this!"

"I'm finally at a point in my life where I'm secure and stable enough to start a family." My face cracked into a wide smile. "But I don't want to do it alone."

✳✳

Our campsite on Winchell Lake in the Boundary Waters was perfect. Helen brought our small group together and we had planned well. Our tents were set far back amidst the trees, and long gently sloped granite rocks led to the water's edge. After dinner, Mindy found the perfect spot to sit: a few warm rocks surrounded by a lapping lake. We watched the sun set, listened to the call of loons, and talked late into the night. We'd already paddled together, matching our strokes perfectly, gliding through both glassy and choppy water. We'd lifted and balanced the heavy canoes, carrying them over the rocky portages. We'd gathered wood and built campfires as the sky turned a deep violet-blue studded with distant sparkling jewels. That night, when our lips met, I knew I was in love.

Everything happened fast after that. A year later, we were living together in Mindy's cozy St. Paul home. We both had flexible schedules—she worked as a professor at the university, and my full-time astrology practice was stable—so we traveled and camped as often as possible. Finally, we took a long-awaited trip to South Point, on the Big Island of Hawaii. An outcropping of barren land, it was windy, empty, and achingly beautiful. I could imagine the gratitude of the first Polynesians who after a long voyage at sea finally spotted land. In the hot sun and powerful wind, I felt my psychic energy open.

I hadn't told Mindy much about this phenomenon, just that sometimes I had intuitive flashes or visions, and knew what was going to happen. I wasn't prepared for what did happen that evening.

As Mindy drove us back to our campground at Mackenzie State Park, I closed my eyes and let myself drift into an altered state. I saw a red pickup truck drive down a dirt road with three men inside. A darkness hovered over the truck. They stopped in front of our tent at the campground and invited us to a party, saying they'd be right back with a keg of beer. A voice inside my head screamed, "Get out!" I woke from the vision startled, my heart pounding, and I almost said something to Mindy, but when I looked at her serene face, it seemed like just a bad dream.

"What a great day," she said, smiling over at me, and took my hand. I nodded, swallowing hard, trying to smile back.

As the water boiled for dinner, I saw it, this time for real. A red pickup truck with three men inside pulled into the campground. Just as in my vision, they stopped in front of our tent and invited us to a party. I saw Mindy's body go rigid, but I played along, hoping they would have to leave to buy beer. They did. As soon as their truck was out of sight, I turned to Mindy. "We're in terrible danger here."

She looked at my face and nodded.

Dragging the entire tent, stakes and all, we heaved our belongings into the back of the rental car. I poured the hot water on the ground, and stuffed everything else in the back seat, my heart racing. I tossed her the keys. "You drive."

"Sure, but tell me what's going on."

"We have to find a motel room." I could hear my voice shaking as I spoke.

When we were safe inside the motel, I sat down on the corner of the soft bed and took a deep breath. Sobs tore out of me with surprising intensity. Mindy wrapped her arms around my shoulders. I leaned into her as if she were a warm shawl.

"You knew something about those guys, didn't you?" she asked.

"I had a vision about them earlier, but thought I was paranoid."

"I never heard fear in your voice like that. What happened in the vision?"

"A voice hollered at me to leave, so when I saw the exact same red truck I knew." A shudder ran through me. "They were going to rape and kill us. I don't know how I know that, but I just do."

The next morning, the roadside café was empty except for a couple seated by the window. We sat on stools at the counter and ordered the special.

"Did you hear the story about the two girls that went missing last night?" the cook asked our waitress. He was plating eggs, potatoes, and toast behind the Formica counter.

"At the Mackenzie campground?" The waitress glanced at us, then put her finger to her lips. "Terrible times."

Mindy squeezed my hand. I looked at her. We didn't say anything; we didn't have to.

21

This Beautiful Being

We moved fast. Within two months, Mindy and I attended a "maybe baby" class for lesbian women. Then we found a reputable fertility clinic. But two years passed with no success. Mindy tried fertility drugs and hormones, but nothing worked. *It's for the best*, I thought. *We're fine as a twosome.* But deep inside, I was sad; one of my dreams for my life had died. I'd often worried what kind of parent I'd be, having grown up in an abusive family. Would I be like Mom, always scolding, finding problems, reducing my child's self-esteem to the nub mine had been? Or would I be able to break our family legacy?

I had just about given up by the time we went to the Bahamas for Mindy's work. She was attending a conference but not presenting, which allowed her to take seminars and find time to relax. I got to fully enjoy the warm tropical sun, comfortable chaise lounges, and rumbling waves. One afternoon, I was lying by the water in a state of deep relaxation when I felt a hand on my shoulder. Mindy squinted down at me. "I've been cramping and spotting."

"Not again." I sat up and rubbed my eyes. The bright sunlight highlighted the dark smudges under Mindy's eyes. No matter how hard this was on me, she had it worse. This last fertilization cycle had been particularly brutal for her because we'd upped the medical intervention. This was the time in her cycle when things usually went wrong. "Let's just stop," I said, voicing my thoughts of the past week. "Our life is good, just the two of us."

Mindy gazed out over the water, and I recognized the stubborn line of her back. "No. I am not giving up."

After we got home, we resumed our trips to the clinic. I'd agreed to six additional fertility treatments, but neither of us had much hope. When the nurse came in, I braced for the usual bad news. As she moved the wand over Mindy's abdomen, something looked different on the screen. "Look," she said, "that's an embryo." I grabbed Mindy's hand.

Our caution slowly gave way to excitement as Mindy enjoyed an easy pregnancy. We furnished the nursery, savored our outings with friends, and were hosted at multiple baby showers. I was glad she hadn't given up; I couldn't remember a time when we were happier, or closer.

At the sound of the first cry, I looked down at my watch to note the time. I would run to my office later and work up a natal chart. I snipped the umbilical cord as arranged, and the nurse wrapped the tiny baby in a towel. "I'll bring her to you in a minute."

"We have a baby!" I said, squeezing Mindy's hand, as tears steamed up my glasses. We sobbed as we held each other. Moments later the doctor set a swaddled baby on Mindy's chest. "How perfect," I said, reaching out with a gentle hand. We had picked two names. "You look like a Della," I said quietly to both of them. Mindy nodded her agreement.

I sat in the nursery rocking Della after the nurse rolled Mindy into recovery. Lou Ann and a couple of friends had smiled at us through the nursery window, and finally my time had come to bond with this tiny, beautiful, fragile being. I cradled Della in my arms and whispered, "You are deeply wanted, and I promise we will always love you." I sighed, shifting my weight in the chair. "I think I've learned enough from the mistakes of my mother."

The early days of parenting passed in a blur of sleepless nights, diaper changes, and learning to be a mom. One morning, as I lifted Della out of the crib, I realized that I'd known love before, but nothing like this. My heart felt broken wide open; there wasn't anything I wouldn't do for this tiny being. Our newborn was colicky, so I used a baby sling and walked endlessly back and forth across the hardwood floor of the nursery. Together we rocked in the rocking chair, listening to Mary Black and Raffi songs on the boom box, as I sang in my off-key voice. And slowly, by tending to the needs of my child, I learned to love myself. Not for personal qualities or accomplishments, but because something deep inside me knew Della deserved all my love, and that I deserved it too.

MINDY AND I changed our work schedules, ate meals on the fly, and napped while Della slept. Putting Della's needs first seemed natural, even instinctual. And that made me wonder: Did my mother feel this way toward me, or was her love divided because there were two of us? Was there another reason I would never know? I wanted to talk to my mom. For the first time in decades I wished she were alive.

DURING THIS TIME, I didn't think much about Lou Ann. Life was full with a baby and our new routines. One afternoon, when Della was finally napping, I called my sister. Her voice sounded a little distant, even chilly, although I knew she was happy for us.

"Elizabeth just put the final touches on the built-ins in our bedroom," she said quietly, "and I want you to see them." She paused. "You haven't been over here in weeks."

I sighed. "It's below zero. Getting Della bundled up and in the car is a big project. Can't you come over today, and I'll see the closets next week?"

She sighed too, long and loud, and began to say something. Just then, I heard Della start to cry on the baby monitor. I felt my body tense. I would never be one of those moms who could just let an infant cry it out. "If you come over, I could take a quick shower while you're here. I haven't showered in two days. Please?" The crying became louder. "Listen, I'll call back in ten."

I knew it was hard for anyone who wasn't a parent to grasp the amount of time and energy an infant takes, and how all-consuming the experience is. Lou Ann came over that day, I got my shower, and we worked things out. But I knew we'd reached another turning point in our relationship. I didn't know how it would end up.

Mindy's and my love for Della never wavered, though our relationship was tested a couple of times when I got a serious injury in a car crash and when Mindy's father died. As Della grew into a toddler, we agreed our family wasn't complete. After taking a weekend workshop on adoption, we had many long conversations and then found a local agency that worked with lawyers in Guatemala, where babies often went right from the hospital into foster families. Permanent placement only took six months. Mindy's sabbatical year was coming up that fall, and we'd be living in France—we hoped—with Della and our new baby.

22

I Already Know Her

"**I**t's so exciting about the baby girl," Lou Ann said. "You must be thrilled."

We'd found a parking spot right in front of Izzy's ice cream shop, one of our favorite meeting places. We'd both loved ice cream and this shop had the best flavors.

"And Mindy's sabbatical came through too." I turned off the car, and we got out.

"I'm happy for you," my sister said, "but nine months is a long time to be gone." She stopped on the sidewalk and turned to face me. "I'm not saying don't go, but I'll miss you."

She opened the door to the shop, and we walked inside. I caught a flash of tears before she turned away. My sister didn't often cry, and I was surprised she was reacting this way. Fifteen years earlier we'd lived in different cities for nine months with only an occasional phone call or visit.

I pushed open the shop's door and inhaled the sugary smell of freshly made waffle cones. "I love that smell, don't you?"

Lou Ann nodded, but kept her eyes averted.

"I'll miss you too," I said, grabbing her shoulder in a brief hug, "but with email we can stay in touch every day."

Instead of replying, she studied the ice cream case and addressed the server. "I'll have a scoop of the chocolate noir in a cup."

I caught the server's eye, "Me too." We got our ice cream, paid, and moved to a table by the door. I let a few minutes pass as we ate. Then I looked up at Lou Ann. "When Ana's adoption is final, sometime in the next two months," I said, "we'll be back here for a week. I hope we can stay in your extra room."

Her face softened. "Of course you can. I can't wait to meet her."

"THEIR PLANE'S ARRIVED at gate C7," Lou Ann said, glancing at the monitor inside the terminal. "C'mon Della, hop on my back." She got on one knee, Della grabbed her around the neck, and we set off down the concourse. We arrived at the gate just as Mindy rolled Ana's stroller into the waiting area. Della slid down to the floor, and we all ran to meet them. As Mindy put down her bags, I unbuckled Ana from the stroller. Mindy had an entire week's head start with our new daughter.

"What's she like?" I asked.

"Wonderful," Mindy said, "eats well, barely cries, already sleeps through the night."

Five-year-old Della touched Ana's hand. "Can I hold her?"

"Sit down," I said, turning to pick up the baby. "I'll put her in your lap."

As I lifted her to my body, Ana looked directly into my eyes and smiled. "Welcome home, sweetie," I whispered in her ear, kissing her soft cheek.

I leaned down and placed Ana in Della's nest of a lap. They both smiled.

"She's so beautiful!" Lou Ann said. "Can I hold her next?" Tears streamed down her cheeks. Once again, I was surprised; I'd never seen Lou Ann cry in public.

"Why the tears?" I moved to stand close to her.

"Somehow I already know her." She inhaled deeply. "And I love her."

Ana completed our family in ways we couldn't have imagined. Della dressed her up and found silly games to make her laugh. I got the royal treatment dispensed to new mothers in France, with people fussing and holding doors open for me and Ana. Women started conversations with me in parks and grocery stores. Our upstairs neighbors offered to babysit and pick up fresh baguettes every day. I never expected to love living in France as much as I did, nor did I expect our new family of four to bond so deeply.

I decided to take a break from my astrology practice during the ten months we were there and just enjoy my new family. But the inner gates still opened without my expecting them. The last time I'd recalled a past life had been with Doris the Reiki healer. This time it happened in downtown Lyon. And it happened in a way that surprised even me.

Lyon's Sunday farmers' market stretched along the Rhone river. Rows and rows of tables overflowed with fresh produce, olives, cheeses, meats, fresh fish, and spices. Almost everything was produced locally. After our first visit, shopping there had become a weekly ritual for us. We followed our noses from one delicious smell to another, and an hour later the bottom of the stroller was filled with mandarins from Spain, local mushrooms, tomatoes, salad greens, and a special "label rouge" chicken from Bresse, a town famous for its chickens.

We packed our provisions and ourselves into our leased minivan and headed back to our apartment. Mindy directed me to follow Rue Fulchiron three blocks and then take a left. As I made the turn, I remembered a recurring dream where I drove through an old European town. The narrow streets and old brick buildings led up a long winding hill. Now in real life I was following the exact same route. "This is wild," I told her, as I accelerated up the hill. "I know this place. I've dreamed it dozens of times."

"Sounds interesting. Merge left up here."

"I know how to get home."

Mindy shrugged. "You're the one without a sense of direction, and you want me to stop giving directions? I don't want to get lost."

"This is different." I felt certain of where to turn and how to go. "Let me check this out. Correct me if I make a wrong turn."

As we pulled into the parking space next to our apartment building Mindy turned to me with a big smile. "I have to say I'm surprised, and not surprised."

It was still a new experience for me, though, and I thought about it for many days after. These openings into another level seemed to come unexpectedly. What were they for? Sometimes I got a clear warning of something dangerous, sometimes a sense of what might happen in the future, sometimes a recall of the past. I didn't talk to Mindy much about it after that day, wanting to keep the feeling to myself. I knew my abilities had saved our lives that evening at the campground: later, we found out that two other women had been raped and murdered by the men in the pickup truck.

I'd come a long way from not having a center, from feeling inferior to Lou Ann, but I still wanted to understand more deeply why these things happened to me. Our time in France became a time to expand my understanding. After the memory of how to drive home in Lyon, the feeling of déjà vu grew stronger. On our weekend drives to small towns and mountain villages, I often felt deeply connected. Our neighbors became good friends, and one of the French moms at Della's school started inviting me to her house, something that never happened to the other Americans we knew living in France. I knew I'd been here before, maybe many times, in other lives, and I never wanted to leave. And even after extending our time there by a month, it was still too soon to return to the States. But I missed my sister. We'd kept in touch, and she and Elizabeth had come for a weeklong visit, but it was time to see her.

23

Twin Tension

While we were in France, Lou Ann had done a lot for me. She'd supervised our renters, taken our injured cat to the vet, found someone to patch a leak in the roof, repaired a leaky faucet, and dealt with other problems. I was glad to see her, grateful for her full-hearted help and her acceptance of my new family. But in the midst of our family reunion a problem emerged.

I MOVED CLOSER to Mindy on the couch and put my hand on her shoulder. "All she wants to do, honey, is pick Della and Ana up from school on Thursdays and take them home for a couple of hours," I said. I glanced out the window where big white flakes of snow were falling, blanketing the trees and shrubs. We were back in our home in Minnesota. "You agreed she could be one of the pick-up people."

She shrugged off my hand, straightening her back and looking down at me. "That was in case of emergency, not every week." She looked out the window. "Ever since that time at their house when Lou Ann walked away leaving Della lying on the bed, I don't trust her. She doesn't have any experience with kids." The worry lines between her eyebrows deepened as she sat forward.

"I didn't have experience with kids either," I sighed. "This is my twin, Mindy. I want our kids to have a relationship with her." The room was growing darker as twilight approached, and I reached over to turn on a lamp. "You know if your sisters lived in town, I'd want them to have special time with the kids."

"That doesn't change the fact that I don't like how your sister drives. She's been in a couple bad car accidents." Her fingers tapped nervously on her leg. "What if she had a crash with our kids in her car?" Tap, tap, tap went her fingers. "Could you live with yourself?"

"She'll be careful if they're in the car. I'll make a point of telling her."

Mindy leaned back, and her body relaxed. "I want them to have family here in town, to know your sister." I moved closer on the couch. "Could we start with a one-month trial?"

The second week, Lou Ann brought the kids inside carrying big sheets of drawing paper.

"Look at what I made," Ana said, her voice full of excitement as she opened her sheet. Inside was a brightly colored scene with blue clouds and multicolored rainbows.

Della showed us a completely furnished, three-dimensional pop-up room made of paper and cutouts. "We had so much fun. Thanks, Auntie Lou Ann," Della said as Lou Ann hugged them goodbye. "See you next Thursday."

As Lou Ann shut the door behind her, Mindy whispered in my ear. "I'm over it. They can go there every week."

MONTHS TURNED INTO years, the seasons changed from white snow to bright flowers, to red and gold leaves, and back. Life was good as we packed our lives with visits to the science museum, camping trips, and family gatherings, which often included Lou Ann and Elizabeth. But underneath the surface, when our families were together, I noticed a subtle tension.

It came to a head one night when we were all sitting together on our back porch. We sat across from Lou Ann and Elizabeth, the air ripe with tension. A few days earlier, Lou Ann had informed me in her kind, therapeutic way that she needed to address something with the four of us.

"I hope this conversation will bring us closer together," Lou Ann began. I remembered her saying something very similar to Dad and Henrietta the day we came out to them, decades ago. Over time they'd accepted who we were, but my memories of that day still rankled. And Lou Ann's approach hadn't gentled their reaction one bit.

"When the four of us spend time together, Mindy," she continued, "I'd like you to show more interest in my life."

Mindy took a sip from her glass of ice water. I could tell her back was still rigid despite the smile on her face. "I am interested, Lou Ann." She paused, putting her glass down. "You remember that I asked you about your work trip?"

"You did," Lou Ann shook her head. "Then you immediately changed the subject to your work."

"Well," Mindy said, a pink color spreading up her neck, "why don't you tell me more about your work? We have time."

I put my hand on Mindy's leg under the table. "Lou Ann's thinking of joining a new clinic."

"I'd love to hear about the new clinic," Mindy said.

There was a long pause. "I'm here to talk about our relationship," Lou Ann said, "not the new clinic." She shot me a look.

"But I'm interested; I really am." Mindy sipped her water again.

They went back and forth on this, and after a bit Mindy just agreed. She would try to show more interest in Lou Ann's life, she said. We finished our water and got up. I could barely hug my sister goodbye.

"Why does she have to make everything into a therapy session?" Mindy asked as we carried the water glasses into the house. "All she has to do is change the subject if she doesn't like what I'm talking about."

I shook my head, not knowing what to say. Even though I'd spent every day with Lou Ann growing up, even though she was as close to me as my own heartbeat, she also confused me. Could something else be bothering her, or did she really need more from Mindy?

THE NEXT TIME Lou Ann and I met, she started our conversation with a declaration: "I wish I'd had kids. That's a big regret." We were sitting on a bench by Lake Calhoun eating turkey sandwiches from a nearby deli. "Watching Della and Ana change and grow has been pure pleasure." She pushed her hair off her forehead. "You're doing such a good job with them."

I wrapped my half-eaten crusts in a napkin and stuck them into the plastic bag. I never got tired of hearing Lou Ann praise my kids, and me. It was hard work parenting differently than our mom. But a nagging bit of worry, or maybe just curiosity, started inside. She'd never spoken of regrets before. Lou Ann wasn't that kind of person—she was self-aware, but focused on the future. I sipped my lemonade and studied her face. She seemed different lately, as if something had happened to her. I probed my inner senses but nothing came forward.

"For instance, I loved watching you explain to Della how to stop whining and be direct. No one taught us that." My sister threw the uneaten part of her sandwich into the bag and stood up. "Want to walk? I have another twenty minutes."

"I'm proud the cycle of abuse we inherited stopped with me," I said, as we moved from the shady bench into the sun, walking along the path that circled the lake. "Both kids push me to the breaking point, but I've figured out ways to cope, not lash out. I've actually been able to keep some of those promises I wrote in my journal as a teen."

Lou Ann smiled. I'd shared those journals with her long ago. "The change started with me studying psychology and you, astrology. Moving past what we knew." She looked out at the lake. "Listen, is that a loon?"

MONTHS LATER THE entire family sat around a long table at my parents' favorite restaurant, It's Greek to Me, listening to balalaika music tinkle in the background. The air smelled of oregano and roasted garlic. On top of our white tablecloth sat plates of pita triangles, bowls of hummus, olives, and a couple carafes of red wine. The adults sipped wine and nibbled on olives, while the kids dipped their pita bread and colored on activity sheets, each with a small box of crayons. Easy conversation flowed around the table as we caught up with each other. It had been a few months since I'd seen Henrietta and Dad, and longer yet since we'd all gotten together. Maybe it was distance, maybe lack of time, or maybe just the uncertainties that still simmered beneath all of our relationships. But tonight we were setting all that aside to celebrate my sister.

Dad tapped on his wine glass with a spoon. "I propose a toast." We lifted our glasses. "To Lou Ann becoming the most educated person in our family." Dad's face gleamed with the unique pride and happiness of a parent who hadn't finished high school. "First she got her master's, and now she just completed a degree in psychoanalysis." He smiled as he looked around the table, his eyes finally resting on my twin. "We are very proud of you." He leaned toward her, and they clinked glasses.

I was proud of Lou Ann too. At lunch the previous week, she'd told me how she'd finally become the therapist she'd always wanted to be. The four-year degree program had been grueling, but worth it, she'd said. I sipped my wine, smiling, trying to be happy for her too. Trying to ignore the feeling that nagged at me.

Every January for the last decade, I had hosted a big astrological predictions event. I'd present a forecast based on what was happening in the heavens in the coming year, analyzing charts of politicians, the economy, the U.S., and then finally made predictions for all twelve zodiac signs. I hired musicians to perform to break up all the talking, and bought delicious baked goods and coffee to sell during intermission. After a few years the event became quite successful, with over 220 people attending. Lou Ann and Elizabeth were there every year, and they always complimented me on all I'd achieved. It was a considerable success in my field.

One year, I thought Dad and Henrietta would enjoy attending, so I got them tickets. I ran into Dad in the crowded auditorium before the program started. I was so excited to see him and hear what he thought of my success. He just said, "All these people paid money to listen to *you?*" with an expression of disbelief on his face. I moved away as fast as I could. The memory still burned.

That night at the restaurant, it turned the wine sour in my mouth. I leaned toward Ana and wrapped my arm around her shoulder.

"What did you draw?" I asked.

"It's a bear," she said. "See the fur?"

"What a pretty brown." I kissed the top of her head.

I caught Della's attention. "You finished the word find, didn't you? I bet you got them all."

No way was I going to let my children suffer the same humiliation, I thought. I wanted them to feel equally loved, equally special, no matter their accomplishments.

I noticed Ana rubbing her eyes. "Sorry to leave," I said, standing up, "but the kids are tired and we have to head home." We gathered our coats, and Lou Ann walked over to give me a big hug.

"Thanks for coming," she said. "It meant a lot."

I was still smarting from the memory. I coughed and pulled away for an instant, then turned and hugged her back.

Part Two

Divergent Paths

**

Joy and sorrow are inseparable. . . . Together
they come, and when one sits alone with you,
remember that the other is asleep upon your bed.
—Kahlil Gibran

24

A Premonition

"Try the quail egg soup," Lou Ann said. "It's good." We sat across from each other in a small Vietnamese restaurant on University Avenue. Since I'd seen her a month ago at the Greek restaurant, she'd lost weight and dark circles dimmed her eyes.

"You look tired." I sipped my tea. "Anything going on?"

She shrugged. "I've had lots of indigestion. After I eat a few bites, I'm full."

"Worried about it?"

"Not really. I figure I'm still recovering from that stupid knee surgery." She coughed into her napkin. "I'll have my physical in a couple months." She looked at me. "Don't worry, I'm fine."

As we stepped outside, small white flakes fell from the sky, leaving a white slippery powder on the sidewalk. I shuffled my feet all the way to the car to keep from falling.

"I'M IN THE hospital," Lou Ann said over the phone a week later. "My doctor admitted me last night."

I stared out my office window, remembering our conversation when she spoke of regrets, and the way she looked at our last lunch. How I'd put aside the nagging feeling, only to have it resurface. Now it came again, frightening in its intensity.

"I'll be there as soon as I can," I promised my sister. It only took fifteen minutes to reschedule the clients for that afternoon and call Mindy. Then I rushed to Fairview Hospital in Edina. But it seemed like hours later when I stood at Lou Ann's bedside and heard the diagnosis.

"I have ovarian cancer." Lou Ann looked small in the white hospital bed, her hair flat in back. "It may have traveled to my lungs."

"What?" I said, taking her hand. I could hardly take it in. Two weeks earlier we had eaten lunch together, and today she had cancer.

She started to cough, her hand slack inside of mine, and as she coughed my lungs ached. Something about the sound reminded me of Mom retching behind the closed bathroom door.

"I'm confused about treatment," she said. "It made Mom so sick." She poured some water from a pink plastic pitcher and sipped. "You predict futures for a living. Tell me what you think."

I shook my head, not meeting her eyes. For the last couple of months, I'd watched Uranus in my chart. The last time it came around Sunsight was bombed and Molly had left me overnight, breaking my heart. Seeing Uranus again made me worry that Mindy and I would be facing struggles. Now I knew it was my twin who would be facing them.

"I want to know," she said. I knew that familiar set to her jaw.

On an impulse, I turned her hand over and glanced at her life line, the one that travels around the thumb. I'd studied palm reading along with astrology in college, and practiced it quite a bit. Her life line stopped short.

"Tell me!"

My mouth felt painfully dry. We'd turned fifty-six on our last birthday. "Your life line is short. It ends in your mid-fifties."

Lou Ann's eyebrows shot up, and paleness spread across her face.

"Shit," I said.

"My night nurse, the one I really like, said I could start hospice now." She sat up straight and adjusted her legs under the covers. A loud silence filled the room. "What if the treatment works?" Her voice echoed the stubborn look on her face. "Anyway, I can't do hospice now because of my clients. I have to help them through this."

Here was the twin I'd always admired. I felt a warmth rise in my cheeks. Then I wondered why she didn't want her own future. "Why is everyone else more important than you?"

She glared at me. "My clients are important. Period." She leaned back into the pillows. "Let's talk about it later," she said. "I'm tired." She closed her eyes, and after a minute her breathing turned steady and even.

As I walked down the long empty hall, listening to the echo of my footsteps, I knew she wouldn't recover. Hospice now or hospice later, her life would end soon. What I didn't know and couldn't even imagine was how I would live without her.

The following day I decided to focus every spare moment on Lou Ann. I rearranged my schedule to be at her doctors' appointments, and I spent time researching ovarian cancer on the web, hoping to find something to offset my premonitions. Instead, I found despair. Ovarian cancer is a deadly disease that runs in families. Lou Ann's and my illnesses tended to mirror each other, so I would probably be next: I'd get sick and not be able to care for her. At Mindy's urging, I booked an appointment with a genetic counselor, who gave me tests. To my relief, they came back negative. "Twins are born with identical genes, but genes change over the course of a lifetime," the counselor told me. "Environmental stimuli can force a gene to mutate slightly, and if that happens, then the person is more susceptible to cancer."

"So I might never develop cancer at all, right?"

"No. Your risk factor is higher because your twin developed the disease."

I left the appointment confused, so I decided to look at our birth charts when I got to work. I started with Lou Ann's. Chiron, the wounded healer, held a prominent position by transit right then. I knew from experience Chiron was often active during clients' illnesses, and because of a small difference between our two charts and the planetoids' erratic orbit, I had a whole year before Chiron came around. I understood this kind of information far better than I understood the results of genetic testing.

I thumbed through the ephemeris next, hoping for more clues. Come spring, both of us had a solar eclipse interacting with the health sector. Seeing that, I slammed the big book closed. Solar eclipses were most often wild cards, bringing darkness before illumination. I wondered what kind of illumination Lou Ann's illness—and likely death—could possibly bring.

25

Caught in the Storm

L ou Ann leaned back in a lounger, eyes closed, her body covered with a fleece blanket. A tube from two IV bags ran into her left arm. She opened her eyes as I approached. "Finally, you're here."

I ignored the sharp edge to her voice. "Of course I'm here." I'd managed to miss the small sign marking the entrance to the clinic three times, driving back and forth on France Avenue, my frustration growing. I took a deep breath and leaned over to kiss her cheek and was surprised by the funny metallic taste in my mouth. This had sometimes happened as kids: I would taste the medicine she was taking.

Lou Ann sipped water from a plastic cup. "Better living through chemistry. That's my new motto." She handed me the cup. "The chemo makes my mouth taste like I've been chewing nails."

I swallowed hard, hating it all. "Where'd you get the water?"

She pointed to a water fountain in a far corner of the treatment room. I went over and drank two cups, fast, almost choking. I wasn't surprised when the metallic taste only intensified. I threw the plastic cup in a trashcan and then slid a chair close to my twin.

"First it's tumors and now chemicals." Her half-smile turned into a grimace. "I'm working really hard to accept all of this."

I gently squeezed her shoulder. "I wish you didn't have to." I could feel her bones though her clothes.

She'd changed so much in just two months, but other than the unease I'd experienced at the Vietnamese restaurant I hadn't let myself notice. *When you're so close, it can be hard to see clearly*, I thought. I watched her lie there, eyes closed, and thought back to a cool, cloudy, fall day when

100

I'd visited her house, following the smell of wood smoke to her backyard pottery studio.

Lou Ann had stood by a big metal tub, feeding sticks one by one into a crackling fire. I marveled as she gauged the temperature of the fire and added the sawdust to the pots cooking there, jumping back as they burst into flame. She loved raku, and she was good at it. Her pottery was prized by her friends and sold at high-end galleries and juried art fairs. At the perfect moment, she put a metal cover over the tub. Later, she'd lifted the metal cover with her mitts and picked up a medium pot with a huge pair of tongs. "Look at this right here." She pointed to a brilliant orange and red design with a nearby streak of deep blue. "That's what they call a flash."

"It looks like the flame that made it." I said as we walked inside for a cup of tea. All through our conversation I thought of the Magician card in the tarot deck, how it symbolized the ability to mix the elements of nature to create something new. Right then I decided my sister was a magician, an alchemist.

"Can you get me more water?" Lou Ann's voice pulled me back to the present. Walking to the water fountain and grabbing a cup, I wished she was magical enough to get well.

Later, as I drove the kids home from school, it started to snow. Big fat white flakes floated onto the ground, blanketing the landscape. I settled the kids inside and went back out to shovel. As I scooped, I bent slightly at the knees, tightening my core to lift the shovel and throw the heavy snow. Each scoop added to the waist-high piles that already accumulated on the sidewalks. The snow was wet and stuck to the aluminum shovel. Frustrated, I kicked the shovel with my boot every once in a while to free the snow, wishing for one of those new, slippery, plastic shovels. As I made my way to the back door, flakes continued to fall behind me, dusting the concrete with a powdered-sugar-like coating.

Inside, I took off my boots, hung up my coat and started scrubbing the potatoes for dinner. I hated that these mundane chores continued to fill my days. With Lou Ann sick, they seemed so inconsequential. My over-developed sense of responsibility got in the way of unshoveled sidewalks and fast food dinners. In the scheme of things what's a snowy sidewalk, I wondered, compared to the illness of my sister? Putting the baking sheet in the oven, I looked at the clock and realized Lou Ann's chemo would just be finishing.

I was certain she and Elizabeth would be caught in the storm.

26

Homemade Pudding and Forgiveness

Weeks passed and Lou Ann's hair fell out, which was expected, but she continued to lose a great deal of weight, which was not. I had to do something, so I made vanilla pudding, a childhood favorite for us both. Mom would bring it to the table still steaming, in matching blue glass bowls. Lou Ann and I would carefully peel off the skin, rolling it onto our spoons and nibbling at it like a delicacy.

Organic eggs, sugar, vanilla, and whole milk went round and round, following my wooden spoon. I shifted my weight from foot to foot, a bit hypnotized, the smell of vanilla strong in my nose. By the next morning it had set with a nice firm skin on top that was golden yellow from all the eggs. I carefully took it from the fridge and placed it on the passenger seat of my car.

In her home hospital bed my sister dipped a spoon into the warmed pudding, blew on it, then nibbled. A big smile broke across her face. "It tastes like childhood. It's good." She grasped my hands in hers, and for a brief moment her face glowed. Then it turned serious. "Remember the big fight we had when you said Mom and Dad favored me?" She leaned even closer, her eyes growing moist. "You were right. I was their golden child, but I didn't want to admit it." Tears spilled onto her cheeks and rolled down to her chin. "I'm so sorry about that. I hate that they made you feel inadequate." She paused as I squeezed her hands. "When I see what a great family you're creating, I realize both Mom and Dad missed the boat on you. They really did." I handed Lou Ann a tissue and she wiped her face. "I waited a long time to tell you that. Maybe too long." I grabbed her into a long, hard hug.

Soon the bowl was empty, and her smile turned into a frown. She pulled the covers aside to show me her swollen, purplish-red calf. "Another blood clot," she said. "Another delay before surgery."

Without surgery, more chemotherapy was the only option, so I met her in the waiting room before her next session. The door opened, and one of the nurses called her name. When Lou Ann stepped on the scale I read her weight: ninety-nine pounds. She'd lost thirty-five pounds. We followed the nurse to a leather recliner, far away from the windows.

After she prepped Lou Ann, the nurse stood up to leave, and I followed her. "Excuse me." She stopped to face me. "My sister's losing too much weight. Why?"

She studied me, and I could see her silently comparing me to my twin. "Everyone responds differently to treatment, and there's a lot we don't know. She gets anti-nausea and anti-inflammatory drugs with the chemotherapy. We're doing everything we can."

Lou Ann dozed in the chair, a blanket draped over her, the bags of chemicals dripping slowly into her arm. Leaning over, I kissed her cheek. She barely stirred. After four treatments she appeared to be getting worse, not better.

Driving down Highway 62, I opened all the car windows and turned the heat up high. Icy wind streamed in, washing out the lingering smell of chemotherapy. I imagined wind pouring through every cell of my body, driving away my fear and hopelessness. As I got out of the car, the sky was a bruised bluish-black, threatening either snow or rain.

I settled in my warm office and reviewed my notes for a few minutes. When my client walked in, she looked different from when we had met a year earlier. There was more gray in her hair and a slight stoop in her posture. She flopped onto my green love seat, kicked off her shoes, and folded her legs under her skirt.

"I've had a terrible month," Jennifer said, picking at a fingernail. "My baby brother passed away from a heart attack four weeks ago. He was only forty-two."

I handed her the box of Kleenex, swallowing hard, trying to be present for Jennifer and not think about Lou Ann.

"He'd been living with us for the last year because he lost his job, and we got really close." Tears leaked out of her eyes and ran down her face. "My husband loved him too."

"It happened suddenly?" I said. "No warning?"

She nodded. "One day we were eating dinner together and laughing over some stupid TV show. The next day I found him in his bed." Jennifer buried her face in her hands. Her whole body shook with sobs.

We sat in silence for a moment. Then she looked up and met my eyes. "So tell me which planets did this."

Thunder rumbled like a freight train off in the distance. "The planets don't make things happen," I said softly. "They just hold up a mirror to help us understand what's going on."

"But I don't understand." She blew her nose. "He built a deck for us over the summer. He seemed strong and healthy."

"It's the transit of Uranus," I said. "It can lead to sudden separations." Thunder boomed overhead, followed by the splat of fat raindrops hitting the roof. "But it also brings changes in consciousness, breakthroughs."

Jennifer's face turned red. "I'm so sick of personal growth I could scream. I just want my brother back. I miss him."

I sat quietly for a moment. "Call me again after a couple months." I put her chart on the table. "No charge."

I watched Jennifer as she walked to her car, rain plastering her hair and clothes. At least I'd get a chance to tell Lou Ann goodbye.

**

The new batch of pudding smelled wonderful. I'd used a whole vanilla bean and organic honey, and packaged it up in a pretty bowl to take to Lou Ann. But she only ate one spoonful before setting it aside.

"I have to tell you my dream." She reached for my arm, and I sank into the chair by her bed. Lou Ann was what I called a strong dreamer. She could get clues in her dreams about things troubling her in the present, and at times dreams helped resolve issues from the past. A distant look came into her eyes as she began to speak. "Mom was in the dream." I began to grimace, but she shook her head. "No, she was very different. She stood inside this vast golden light with her arms stretched wide, wearing the most loving expression on her face. I suddenly understood how much she loved us. That she'd always loved us." My sister's eyes filled with tears. "I forgave her completely."

My heart ached with the possibility of this. I'd started to forgive Mom, understanding more about how her life was hard and remembering occasional sweet times, but too many bad memories piled up inside me, things my mother had done to us before she died and left us all alone. I did manage to say, "That's wonderful," and mean it. "What do you think the dream means?" I asked. Her four years of training in psychoanalysis included dream interpretation too; it was a big part of her work with clients.

"Aside from the obvious, about forgiveness, it told me that I won't be alone after I die." She sighed, and I knew how much this meant to her. Even with her focus on spirituality, my sister still had moments of fear about what would happen. She paused and added, "Mom loved us, even though she couldn't show it."

I had taken after my mother in many ways. As a child, I pretended to be the mom in childhood games, and as a young adult I found myself erupting in rage over the smallest things, just like her. I assumed I'd have those rages all my life, just as she did, even though I didn't want to. With the help of therapy, I gradually changed. My sister's temper, never as volatile as mine, mellowed as well.

The biggest test came when I chose to become a parent. Each kid tested me in different ways. That's when I would hear Mom's critical, shaming voice in my head and feel her rage in my body. Mostly, I managed to grit my teeth and stay frozen in silence until I regained control.

I remembered Della at three, rebelling constantly, questioning everything. One day, after Mindy left for work, I'd been trying to get Della ready for preschool. I felt rushed, wanting to get to the office and deal with a backlog of work. After the fifth squirming refusal to put on a coat, I screamed a bitter threat. As soon as the words were out of my mouth, I regretted them. Della's sweet face crumpled as if physically struck, and tears followed.

I promised myself it would never happen again.

THE PLAYGROUND BEHIND the kids' elementary school was full of waiting parents on a Friday in early June. School would end the following Tuesday, and I could almost feel the hum of anticipation. The sun was warm, and I stretched out on a bench to watch for my children. Soon the closing bell jangled, and the doors opened. Immediately I was surrounded by kids of all ages, running, yelling, laughing, and playing.

Ana ran up to me. "Can I stay and play, please?" she asked. I knew Della had made plans to go home with a friend, so off Ana went as I chatted with one of the dads. The breeze was full of sweetness from a nearby flowering crab apple tree, and he was entertaining me with a funny story about his youngest daughter when a friend of Ana's grabbed my arm.

"Ana's been hurt."

I ran over. Ana sat on the ground next to a tube slide, howling with pain and fright. Blood ran down her forehead and along the side of her face. I grabbed tissues from my bag and held them to her head, then gently lifted her onto my lap. One of the teachers brought over a wet towel and a small ice pack. When I cleaned the blood away, I saw there was a small gash above her right eyebrow.

"Keep pressure on it," the teacher said.

"What happened, honey?" I rubbed my daughter's back, and her sobs quieted to hiccups.

"A sixth grader ran into me, and I hit my head."

A boy with short blond hair was standing to the side, nervously pulling on his T-shirt. I motioned him over. He came, barely looking at us. "I didn't see you there," he mumbled. "Sorry."

"She's okay," I said. "Accidents happen."

"Take the ice pack with you," the teacher said, as I handed her the bloody towel.

I got Ana into her car seat and home, but I couldn't stop the bleeding. I knew the nearest emergency room was fifteen minutes away, so I sped there after talking on the phone to a nurse. We got immediate care, first to numb the area, and a bit later to put in stitches. Ana was stoic throughout. Two hours later, we arrived back at the house, Ana proudly showing off her stitches to Della and Mindy. Her badge of courage.

As I tucked my warrior daughter into bed that night, I felt grateful her injury was minor enough to make her proud instead of afraid. I remembered Mom yelling at Lou Ann when she broke her leg in sixth grade, telling her she was so clumsy. Lou Ann, grimacing from the pain, tried to be quiet and careful with her crutches and didn't ask for much, so as not to incite Mom's anger. Ana's stitches would dissolve in a week, and soon this trauma would be forgotten, I thought as I read her a bedtime story and kissed her goodnight.

Linda and Lou Ann,
four months old

Linda and Lou Ann,
four months old

Linda and Lou Ann,
nine months old

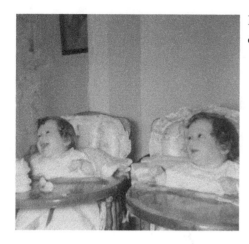

Linda and Lou Ann,
one year old

Linda and Lou Ann,
two years old

Linda and Lou Ann,
two years old

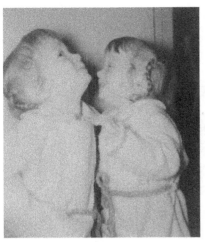

Lou Ann and Linda,
three years old

Lou Ann and Linda,
three years old

Linda and Lou Ann,
four years old

Lou Ann and Linda,
five years old

Lou Ann and Linda,
eight years old

Lou Ann and Linda,
nine years old

Lou Ann and Linda,
nine years old

Lou Ann and Linda,
twelve years old

Lou Ann and Linda,
twelve years old

Lou Ann and Linda's
b'nai mitzvahs

Lou Ann's wedding

Lou Ann on a day hike

Linda and Lou Ann's fortieth birthday

Lou Ann and Linda's
fiftieth birthday

Lou Ann's Natal Chart
Wed. September 1, 1948, 5:23 pm CST +6:00, Minneapolis, MN
44°N58'48" 093°W15'49"
Geocentric, Tropical, Koch, Mean Node

Linda's Natal Chart
Wed. September 1, 1948, 5:47 pm CST +6:00 Minneapolis, MN
44°N58'48" 093°W15'49"
Geocentric, Tropical, Koch, Mean Node

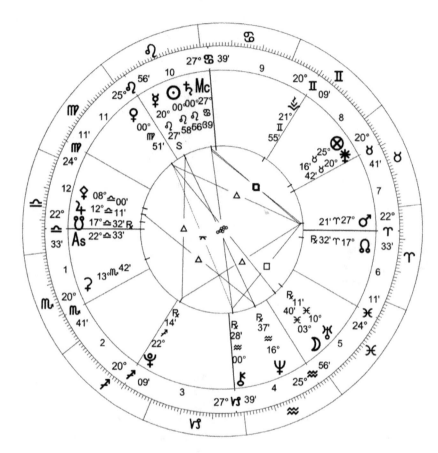

Lou Ann's Death Chart
Sat. July 23, 2005, 1:05 pm CDT +5:00, St. Paul, Minnesota
44° N56'40" 093°W05'35"
Geocentric, Tropical, Koch, Mean Node

21

Liberating the Unlived Spirit

Three months passed with bi-weekly chemotherapy sessions and doctors' visits for Lou Ann. Even though I went to the office most days, my heart was with my twin. One morning our phone conversation set off my alarm bells; I had a sense of my sister's situation worsening, a crisis coming. I tried to still my fears but ended up calling her back, reaching her after dinner.

"I think you should be in the hospital." I knew I sounded irrational as I braced myself for disagreement. She hated hospitals, but I knew something was wrong.

"Me too."

"Really?" I was surprised and relieved. "I'll arrange it." I paged Lou Ann's oncologist. "You've got to admit my sister right now," I said. "Something is very wrong."

"What could be wrong?" Once again I sensed her doctor's indifference, his dislike of me. "Her numbers are fine."

My urgency prompted me to lie: "She's stopped eating. Two days now."

He exhaled loudly. "Bring her in. My shift is over, but I'll stay to make check-in easy."

As I pulled up under the red emergency sign, I saw my sister's tan Toyota parked by the door. I knew she was inside, so I hurried to find a parking spot. Time crawled until I arrived on the eighth floor. The nurse looked up from her computer.

"Dr. Gerhardt is waiting for us," I told her. Then I heard a familiar cough and turned to see Lou Ann. She gave me a feeble smile.

The nurse frowned. "The doctor just left." She studied me, as if assessing the seriousness, then nodded. "Go sit with your sister, and I'll page him. He can't be far."

Lou Ann was shivering, arms wrapped around her body. "I hate hospitals," she coughed again, "but I'm glad you made me come." Her eyes were shadowed and bloodshot, but in spite of her appearance something inside of me relaxed. At least we were here now, with people who knew how to take care of her.

The nurse walked over with a blanket, and Lou Ann reached for it, wrapping it around her shoulders. "The doctor isn't answering yet." She didn't look at me, just helped my sister wrap the blanket around her shoulders. "I'll keep trying."

"Please," I said. I pulled over three hard-backed chairs and pushed them together. "Can you get some pillows?" The nurse nodded. Soon we had Lou Ann curled up on her side, pillow under her head, the blanket cozy around her. She closed her eyes. I saw Elizabeth, Lou Ann's partner, coming off the elevator. They'd been together for thirty years, and tonight I was glad to see her.

"Where's Dr. Gerhardt?" she asked, scanning the room.

"The nurse is paging him." I pitched my voice low so Lou Ann wouldn't hear me. "Something is wrong, I know it."

She sighed. "Without the doctor it could take hours to get checked in. We should go down to emergency."

I nodded toward a quietly sleeping Lou Ann. "Let's wait."

Elizabeth sighed again and nodded. I couldn't imagine what she must be going through; I saw the deep sadness in her eyes and felt a flood of compassion. She sat next to Lou Ann, and I went over to the big windows that looked out over the western horizon. A red sun hung in the sky surrounded by crimson clouds, and the nearby glass buildings reflected its fiery fury. I made myself take deep calming breaths until the final bit of light vanished. Then came darkness, pressing on the windows with a terrible weight.

Finally, the nurse reappeared. "We have a room for Lou Ann." I gently woke my sister; Elizabeth took one arm, I took the other, and we followed the nurse down the hall. Finally there was a flurry of medical activity around her bed, although no doctor yet. But once Lou Ann was settled, I decided to go. She barely glanced at me as I said goodbye.

On the way to the car I called home, my fury at the doctor's broken promise still burning. At Mindy's suggestion I paged the doctor again.

He called me back immediately. "What's wrong?" he asked.

"She's been admitted," I said, my voice trembling from anger. "Where the hell were you?"

"We agreed to meet first thing tomorrow."

"Bullshit!" I yelled. "You agreed to meet us tonight. She's in crisis, and you're not there."

I waited through a long pause. Finally, he cleared his throat. "You can't talk to me like this . . ." he began.

"The hell I can't!" I exploded. "First thing tomorrow I'm filing a formal complaint against you." I ended the call and sat there until my body stopped shaking, then I drove home.

Lou Ann called from the hospital the next morning. "The doctor called it a precipitous drop in my hemoglobin." Her voice sounded strong, normal.

"What does that mean?" I watched the kids get their school backpacks together.

"They gave me blood transfusions all through the night." She paused. "If I'd been home, I could have suffered complications."

Was she thanking me, in a roundabout way, for my alarm? I knew what I'd done was right, and she'd agreed. It was unlike Lou Ann to talk in riddles. I wanted to ask her more, but I looked at the kitchen clock. "I'm taking the kids to school now," I said, "but I'll call later." As I drove, her words sunk in. Lou Ann would have died last night without the transfusions. It would have been much more than complications; I would've lost her. I knew that deep in my cells.

When I got to my office, I took out both of our charts and put them side by side on my desk. The differences, as in the birth charts of all twins, were few. Because of the twenty-four minutes between our birth times, our rising signs, or ascendants, were nine degrees apart on the wheels before me. I'd studied birth charts of other twins, always curious about the degrees of separation between two souls gestating within the same womb and born together, and I knew that most showed closer alignment to each other than Lou Ann's and mine. For professional astrologers, a nine-degree difference in birth charts is small, but in predictions it can be all important.

I looked closer. Chiron, the archetype of the wounded healer, was active for Lou Ann on her chart during the coming months. Not on mine. I pulled out a book on Chiron by one of my favorite authors, Brian Clark, and found the paragraph I'd read so many times: "Chiron, with his incurable wound . . . chooses death to relieve his suffering. . . . Hopefully what chooses to die are the misshapen and inauthentic parts of self. The initiation could then help reorder priorities, relinquish what is no longer appropriate or authentic and liberate the unlived spirit."

During her illness, especially as it worsened, an inner healing started in Lou Ann that liberated her unlived spirit. Like the wisp of smoke after you blow out a candle, it snuck in between moments of nausea, doctors' appointments, and bad news. I saw a new serenity on her face, noticed a looser posture in her body, and heard a soothing quality in her voice. She spent more time listening to inspiring music and reading Buddhist teachings. Underneath it all lay an acceptance of death, a willingness to leave behind parts of her that were unnecessary and inauthentic. I saw her transform from wounded healer into something far more illuminated.

Later I would come to understand that to survive her death I would have to do the exact same thing.

28

The Golden Light

I never found out what had caused the dangerous drop in hemoglobin that almost killed my twin, but over the following weeks the clotting issue resolved itself and surgery was scheduled. On a warm spring day, I drove Lou Ann to her pre-op physical. Right before we left she shared another dream. In the dream she was holding hands with Elizabeth and me as we all floated up toward the place she called "the golden light." Her excitement at sharing this wondrous place with us was palpable; this was where she heard serene, beautiful music and felt no pain. In the dream it only took a moment until we hit a barrier and Lou Ann was forced to let go of our hands.

"I really wanted you to see that place," she said, her face full of longing.

"Me too." It sounded wonderful, but in my mind it loomed as a doorway to death.

**

Joggers, skateboarders, and bicyclists in shorts and tank tops all moved along on Bde Mka Ska's paved paths as we made our way to the clinic. Lou Ann wore jeans and a long-sleeved sweater in spite of the eighty-degree heat. Her shoulder bones and elbows jutted through her sweater and her light-weight summer cap sat slightly askew on her bald head. Chemo was making her sick, but I thought it was extending her life.

"Life is for the living, isn't it?" My sister stared out the window at the people enjoying the day, her voice a little strained. "I can't imagine running, or even walking, around part of that lake."

My hands tightened around the steering wheel. Maybe she wanted to sit outside in the sunshine, not face this next step. "You still want to do this?"

"I'm desperate for it. I can feel the tumors growing at night." She grimaced. "I really don't stand a chance without surgery."

We knew where to park; everything had become eerily familiar. I nodded to the receptionist who signed us in. A nurse appeared, clipboard in hand, to escort us down the hall. Lou Ann turned away when I offered my arm; instead she used her right hand to steady herself on the wall as she walked. At the scale, the green dots settled into the shape of numbers: eighty-nine pounds. I could barely look. Only four months earlier, my sister had been a healthy hundred and thirty-four. The nurse opened a door to a small exam room. Dr. Wright, the on-call doctor, was six feet tall with a few sparse hairs clipped close to his scalp. He stood in the doorway, studying Lou Ann. "You're here to get approval for home hospice?" he ventured.

My sister straightened in her chair, her eyebrows shooting up. "Not at all," she said. "I'm here for a pre-op physical. My oncologist has set a date for surgery early next week." In her I saw a spark of my stubborn sister.

The doctor nodded, not looking at me. He patted the exam table. Lou Ann grunted as she hoisted herself up. "Your blood pressure is low normal." He jotted numbers onto her chart, then moved the stethoscope around on her back and chest. "Your heart and lungs sound fine. Your weight is unacceptable, but since the surgery is scheduled, I'll sign off on it." He looked directly at her. "Drink a full sixty-four ounces of Gatorade the day before surgery to stabilize your electrolytes." He walked out, leaving us silent. She moved off the exam table, refusing my help.

The joggers around the lake were sparse as I turned the car toward home. We were halfway there when Lou Ann finally spoke: "Can you believe he wanted to kill me off like that?"

"You look frail." I said it softly. I knew why the doctor had made the mistake. Anyone would, seeing her.

"The surgery will make me better." She turned to the window. "The surgery will turn the tide." It was the same voice she used with the doctor, but I could hear the fear behind it.

Two days later I brought over the Gatorade. Two large bottles, enough to energize a whole team of joggers. I poured her a glass, but she patted the quilt on her bed. "Come lie down with me," she said. "I need you closer, sis."

My heart warm and hurting, I positioned myself on top of the covers between her and the dozing cat. Lou Ann took my hand. Her skin was warm and dry. "Yesterday Paul and Mary came over and cleaned the entire house. Mary dusted each leaf on every plant, and Paul scrubbed the floors on his hands and knees. Then he took the rugs outside on the clothesline and beat them with a broom."

"People really love you." I gently squeezed her hand.

"What a shame I have to be so sick to let in the love." Her voice was tinged with tears. "How sad is that?" Her eyelids fluttered, and a small shudder ran through her body. "I'm tired. I'll drink Gatorade in a few minutes."

Over many years I'd watched an apparently happy Lou Ann enjoying affection and love from her friends and family. I also watched her taking care of everyone in her life: me, her clients, family, friends, and Elizabeth. Now she was sad at all the love, and that surprised me. Maybe all her giving had been a substitute for a deeper level of receiving. Would letting in the love nourish her finally, even help her survive the surgery?

I got up carefully from the bed. The cat yawned and blinked at me, but my sister didn't stir.

The following day Elizabeth paced around my kitchen. She'd stopped over to return our stockpot and asked if I had time for a cup of tea. I said no, I had errands. Elizabeth's requests for "five minutes" usually turned into hour-long conversations, and I was exhausted from being up in the night with Ana.

"Why is it you have so much time for Lou Ann, but when I need support you're unavailable?"

I took a deep breath. "I can barely imagine how hard Lou Ann's illness is for you, but please find other people to lean on right now," I said. "I know you have lots of friends."

I was confused. Elizabeth and I had a history of shared family gatherings but never sought each other out to talk. In fact, often I sensed some underground tension or competition when the three of us spent time together.

"It's clear you don't care about me." She stopped her pacing and stood directly in front of me. "You'll drop everything to run out and pick up Gatorade for Lou Ann, but you can't find a few minutes for me?"

I stood up straighter and put my hands on my hips. "Lou Ann needs the electrolytes to prepare for surgery. Whatever improves her chance of survival takes priority." I took a deep breath. "She almost failed the pre-op physical."

Elizabeth glared at me as she walked to the front door. "I'll see myself out." The door closed behind her with a shush, the weather stripping making it impossible to slam.

21

Intensive Care

"I've got my A team working with me today, Lou Ann," Dr. Gerhardt said. "We're expecting a great outcome." Despite my protestations, he was still on the case and performing her surgery. I knew how tough it would be to change doctors at this stage. And in spite of our conflict, Elizabeth and I would stay at the hospital throughout Lou Ann's surgery. Lou Ann caught my eye as they rolled her bed away and gave me a thumbs-up. I waved to her and imagined myself standing by the ocean as the tide turned. I wanted to believe with her force of conviction that surgery would lead to recovery.

I wished our horoscopes indicated otherwise. I'd looked at the charts again the day before, and Lou Ann's showed uncertainty and chaos. No matter how many times I checked or studied my ephemeris, it was clearly there: death was in her future, separation in mine. It made me wonder how much free will we actually have. This was a question my clients often asked. I told them the stars helped us know potentials, so we could prepare, and everything in the chart acted symbolically. But what if the future was dark and disturbing? Would I fight, as Lou Ann was, or surrender and accept?

The waiting room was crowded with people talking, eating packaged muffins, and reading newspapers. In the corner a TV flashed the local weather. I took out the new book I was trying to read, *The Da Vinci Code*, but the tense story was no match for what was happening in real life. Time dragged. After an hour I decided to go outside and walk around the small park next to the hospital. The air smelled damp, reminding me of a day several years earlier.

My sister and I had been walking in a park like this one, talking about the ongoing mystery of our mother. Something had happened to Mom in her childhood, we both suspected it. Something bad. But she never talked about it. It came to our awareness that she was troubled. It was a dawning awakening that had hit us at different times in our lives.

"I figured it out in third grade," my sister told me that day, the breeze blowing strands of hair onto her cheek.

I brushed them away. "I was clueless until my twenties, even later."

"Didn't you notice when we went to the cousins' house how Aunt Dianne let them be kids? I mean their rooms were messy, they were loud, and they laughed all the time. They were kids being kids. Not like how we were with Mom."

I glanced over at my sister's serene face. "I remember Mom made a point of telling me how Dianne let her kids act like wild animals."

". . . and you wanted to be good, right?"

"I felt so desperate for her love I'd do anything." I stopped and looked at my twin. "How did you know something was wrong with Mom and not you?"

Lou Ann looked me directly in the eyes. "I can't explain, but I knew it was her problem."

"What went wrong for her," I mused, looking out over the soft green landscape, "that could never be fixed?"

HOURS LATER DR. Gerhardt appeared in the waiting area. He pulled off his blue surgical cap and came over to me and Elizabeth, smiling at her but not looking at me. "It was an optimal debulking," he said. "We removed two big tumors and sent biopsies to the lab." He paused. "Within a week, we'll know exactly what kind of cancer we're dealing with."

"What a relief," Elizabeth said.

"You got it all?" I asked.

"There are always malignancies smaller than a grain of sand that we can't get surgically." He ran his hand over his face. "She'll get more chemotherapy, the right type for her tumors."

"Can we go see her?" Elizabeth and I asked, almost at the same time.

"Not yet. I'll send someone to get you soon."

Two hours later a nurse gave us directions to intensive care. The doctor hadn't said anything about intensive care, I thought as we walked silently down a long hall to an oversized bay crowded with bulky machines. Above Lou Ann's bed, screens pulsed and glowed; sickly green light spilled onto her skin. Her hands fluttered around her mouth like frightened birds as she motioned to the nurse to remove the breathing tube.

My lungs filled with sudden pain; I stopped to catch my breath. Elizabeth hurried to her side.

"The surgery was a total success." Elizabeth's voice was loud, as if Lou Ann were hard of hearing, but I knew she was working to be positive. Lou Ann nodded. She pointed again to the tube in her mouth.

"Can you take that out?" I asked the nearest nurse.

"We need the results from a blood test first."

Lou Ann's eyes settled on me. She pantomimed writing. I found a pen and a scrap of paper in my bag and handed them to her. She scribbled something and handed the paper to me.

"What time is it?" I read out loud.

I looked at my watch. "8:20."

She motioned writing again.

"A.m.?"

"8:20 at night." I swallowed. "You went into surgery fourteen hours ago."

Her body slumped back and she closed her eyes. Elizabeth took her hand and began to tell her word-for-word what the doctor had said.

I found a restroom down the hall and shut myself into a stall. Sobs poured from my chest; I could feel how close to death she'd been. I stayed there until I was calm and went to say goodbye.

One long streak of pink cloud lingered against the night sky as I drove home. Lou Ann's hope was like that cloud, a piece of brightness fighting against the night. I followed it until it faded into darkness.

Two days later, Lou Ann graduated from intensive care into a regular room. I relaxed, knowing her recovery was underway, but that changed later in the day when I heard her coughing as I walked down the hall. The sound grew harsh as I entered her room. I put my hand on her back. "Can't they give you something?"

She sipped water until her breathing settled. "Cough medicine with codeine is on the way." Her voice still sounded weak, but the tone of her skin was pink and her hair was clean and brushed. All the tubes and big machines were gone, and her room was full of balloons, flowers, and cards.

"No need to stay," she coughed into a tissue. "I'm not good for much."

"No matter, I'm staying." I settled into a plastic chair and pulled a book out of my bag.

Soon a nurse walked in with a small, plastic medicine cup filled halfway with red liquid. A few minutes later Lou Ann's coughing stopped, her eyes closed, and she fell asleep. She'd spent fourteen hours in surgery, and now she was regaining her strength. She was eating, drinking, and looking more like herself.

I put down the book and closed my eyes, listening to her gentle breathing. I found myself matching her rhythm almost unconsciously: her exhale as I breathed out, her slight inhale as I breathed in. The muted sound of tinny voices over the sound system and the squeak of soft-soled shoes in the corridor outside faded as I breathed with my twin. My body rose and fell against the chair, heavy and relaxed, as I imagined our hearts beating in unison stretching back to conception. This bond was so intimate, so deep. I promised myself I'd remember this moment forever.

30

A Dream of Dust

A week later when I visited my sister at her house, I was surprised to see her dressed and sitting in the shade on their back deck. I couldn't remember the last time I'd seen her outside. She sipped a tall glass of iced tea and nibbled from a plate of grapes, cheese, and crackers.

"You seem much better." I pulled up a brown wicker chair.

"I am." She smiled. "Surgery did the trick." She pointed to the cheese plate. "Help yourself."

I took a piece of cheese and chewed it slowly. She looked so different, and hope surged through me. "Remember me telling you about the family trip we'd planned for this summer?" I began. "I wondered . . ."

"Go," she said, her voice strong. "I want you to have that time with Mindy and the kids. I'm better, and you deserve some time off." She interrupted when I opened my mouth to speak. "Don't argue," she said. "We can email and talk on the phone."

**

As I sat in a stuffy French phone booth, my eyes drifted past the dirty glass, lingering on the rows of colorful beach towels and families playing in the surf. *Lou Ann's advice was good*, I thought. *I'm glad we came.* I entered the ten-digit calling card code followed by her phone number. Under Mindy's watchful eye, Della and Ana built sculptures with their plastic shovels and pails, their laughter ringing across the sand. We were all having a wonderful time in this little beach town, Le Lavandou. At least they were. A big part of me was on the other side of the ocean, with my sister.

The sound of her voice reassured me. She sounded cheerful. I pressed the receiver to my ear. "You sure you don't mind me being so far away?"

"Hearing about your adventures is the highlight of my day." The phone line whined with feedback. "I'm boring. It's either home or clinic." During our last conversation she'd told me her tumor-specific chemotherapy was three times a week, unlike the earlier bi-weekly treatment. "The new treatment makes me feel like shit."

I didn't know what to say about her feeling worse, so I changed the subject. "Della and Ana found some tiny pink shells today, and now they want to bring the whole beach home."

Lou Ann chuckled. "I'd like some shells from France. What else have you been doing?"

"We ate beignets earlier, the kind dusted with crunchy sugar and filled with gooey Nutella."

Lou Ann laughed a genuinely happy laugh. "I love Nutella."

"I wish I could bring you one." I changed positions and caught sight of the aqua blue Mediterranean. "It was so messy we ended up eating sand too."

"I'm thrilled for you," she said. Her voice was quiet, sincere, and I felt a surge of love for her. "Tell me about those open-air markets."

As we chatted, I relaxed. This might work. I would enjoy my family while Lou Ann got the treatment she needed. Then I'd be home in a couple of weeks—renewed, refreshed, and ready for what came next.

Three days later I sat in a phone booth in the small town of St. Rémy. We'd left the cool breezes of the Mediterranean, and Provence was in the middle of a heat wave.

"I'm nauseated all the time," Lou Ann said, her words coming out in short bursts. "Everything I eat tastes like sand."

I'd called, looking forward to hearing about her progress, but she was much worse. Suddenly, unexpectedly, she was getting worse. *Why weren't the doctors taking care of this?* I thought, panicked. My bright memory of those Nutella beignets faded to dull gray. The trip had been a mistake; she needed me.

I started to speak, but she broke in. "I need to get off. Sorry."

I heard a click. The dial tone wavered across the ocean. I returned the phone to the cradle and made my way out of the booth, stumbling over the metal threshold. Cursing and crying, I walked back to our apartment. I told Mindy about Lou Ann's quick decline, and she suggested we walk to town, do something to lighten the mood. There wasn't anything I could do, she reasoned, not at this very moment. Elizabeth was there helping. I reluctantly agreed.

After slathering ourselves with sunscreen, we headed down the front walkway where heat rose from the asphalt in waves.

"I'm hot," Ana's voice whined. I blinked hard, not sure if it was sweat or tears running down my face.

"Me too." Della pulled on my arm. "Can't we take the car?"

"It's good to spend time outside, kids." Mindy forged ahead. "We'll have ice cream in town."

At the end of the block we came to a round stone fountain. Water rushed out of three small metal tubes and streamed into a deep, circular, stone basin. I untied the bandanna from my neck and dipped it into the water. It was icy cold. Draping the wet bandanna around my neck, I felt the delicious coolness trickle down my back. I handed the kids and Mindy their bandannas from my backpack. We all dipped and draped. Soon there were smiles and eagerness to find more fountains.

A couple hours later we stopped at a bistro famous for ice cream and gelato. Mindy's idea was working: I hadn't thought of Lou Ann for most of our fountain adventure, but seeing the pictures on the menu reminded me of how much she loved gelato, and there were over thirty flavors here. I picked a double scoop of her favorites, hazelnut and chocolate.

"This bite is for me. This bite is for Lou Ann," I said to myself as I ate, trying to send waves of pure pleasure to her across the ocean.

IN SPITE OF the day's long walk, once night fell, I couldn't sleep. I moved to the unoccupied bedroom in our rented apartment. I must have drifted off, because hours later I woke up suddenly, my left side burning with pain. I'd dreamed Lou Ann and I were five-year-old conjoined twins. My left leg and arm were joined to her right leg and arm. Maneuvering together was easy, and I liked the sound of our footsteps echoing double as we skipped up and down the long bright halls of a hospital. At the end of the hall Mom took us into an exam room and introduced us to the doctor. He was tall and stern, and as he looked us over a scowl spread across his face.

"This is no longer viable." Without hesitation he took a scalpel out of his white coat and sliced us apart.

"That hurt!" I yelled as Lou Ann shrank into a small ball and turned to dust.

I sat up in bed. I'd had a dream like this right after Lou Ann was hurt in a car accident years earlier. In the dim bedroom I grabbed for the phone and my phone card, calculating the time difference. Usually on a Saturday afternoon she'd be home, but there was no answer. I called her friend Judith. No answer there either. I made my way down to the tiny kitchen and paced in the dark. At sunrise, I woke Mindy to tell her the dream. Together we decided to wait and keep phoning.

Finally, later in the day, our phone rang. We'd given our numbers in France to everyone close to Lou Ann, in case something happened. And it had. Judith's voice was somber.

"Lou Ann spent last night at the hospital," she said. "Her lung collapsed."

I groped for a chair. Mindy stood by me, listening. I could hear the kids playing in the next room. "Her lung?" I breathed.

"She stopped breathing during a chemo treatment," Judith said. "They got her stabilized right away, and she's home. She's fine."

I couldn't imagine that Lou Ann was fine, but I'd grown to trust Judith. We talked for a few more minutes, until she convinced me there was nothing I could do.

"Alright," I said. "Call me if anything changes."

It took everything I had to not take the next plane home, to stay with the family plan to continue our vacation in the French Alps. But I couldn't stop my feelings. All day I was distracted and crabby. During our hike I yelled at Della and Ana when they strayed too far off the path, and the glory of the mountains, so breathtaking the day before, seemed ordinary. By the end of our hike, I couldn't wait to get back to our apartment, eat something, and drown in the oblivion of sleep.

The phone woke me with a shrill ring. I flipped on the table lamp. The clock read 4:15 a.m. "It's Judith. I have bad news."

A wave of nausea swept through me. "What is it?"

"Lou Ann is much worse. She decided to start hospice." I heard her muffled sobbing. "Come home."

I woke Mindy. She went to make flight arrangements. I stumbled outside onto the balcony and sat on the wooden bench. It was damp from the rain, but the air was warm and smelled of pine forests. Off in the distance I watched lightning play between two mountain peaks. Brilliant flashes illuminated the clouds as muffled thunder followed. The town below lay silent as I listened to the sound of my beating heart.

"Wait for me, sis," I whispered across the distance. "I'm coming as fast as I can."

31

Seashells and Pink Hearts

We started packing around 5:00 a.m., turning on a small table lamp against the darkness outside. In spite of our whispered attempts to stay quiet, within minutes both kids were in the living room, rubbing their eyes. We sat on the couch and invited each of them to climb into one of our laps. I worked hard to speak over the lump in my throat. "We're flying home today. Auntie Lou Ann is starting hospice." I swallowed. "That means she'll die soon." Tears leaked down my cheeks. Both kids and Mindy started crying. "It's good to cry," I said. "Just let it out."

The four of us sat huddled together, faces wet with tears, holding each other as the rain gently pattered against the windows. Wiping my eyes, I wished I'd had a different childhood, a childhood where I'd been told people die, where I'd been allowed to feel my grief. At least I was able to give that gift to my children.

The trip home lasted twenty brutal, sleepless hours. Rolling the suitcases into our hot stuffy house, I imagined myself running into our room and falling into my own bed, sleeping hours of uninterrupted sleep. "Just leave the suitcases, honey." Mindy pecked my cheek. "Go see your sister."

As I coaxed the car to life, sweat rolled down my face and neck. I brushed it away with a damp hand until the air conditioning started to work. Before I drove up the long hill to Lou Ann's house, I found myself taking extra time at each stop sign, remembering that Judith told me to prepare myself for an emaciated Lou Ann.

The front door stood open, so I went in to climb the flight of stairs to her room. Halfway up, I had to stop to catch my breath, my body heavy with fatigue and dread.

There she was, in a hospital bed by the windows, with the rise and fall of her chest the only thing to assure me she was alive. Wiry blue blood vessels popped through the pale, parchment-like skin that covered her face and forehead. Slate-colored shadows surrounded her sunken eyes. Every bone in her face and neck stood out in harsh relief. She looked exactly like the people we saw in the Sunday school films of Holocaust survivors.

Panic rose, hot and fluttering inside my chest, as I walked toward the bed. If I didn't know this was Lou Ann, I wouldn't recognize her. No one could mistake us for each other. She slowly turned her head and looked at me. "Thank God you're here," she exhaled slowly. "I can die now."

I leaned over to kiss her cheek. "I got home as soon as I could."

"I know." Her voice was flat. Her eyes were flat. I searched her face for a glimmer of a smile or a welcome. Nothing.

"I brought you French chocolate . . ." I noticed Lou Ann's usual mug and empty plates were missing. The light in the room dulled as the air conditioner hummed louder. ". . . but you're not eating anymore."

"Right." Lou Ann closed her eyes.

Lou Ann stayed silent as I talked with Elizabeth's daughter and son-in-law, who'd arrived earlier that day. Her eyes followed the voices, but I sensed a deep detachment inside her. Elizabeth walked in and greeted me. She began to explain Lou Ann's condition and what the hospice nurse told her, but after a few minutes my eyes kept closing, and I knew that I wouldn't be safe to drive home unless I left now.

I leaned over the bed. "I'll be back tomorrow."

She moved her hand from under the covers and grasped mine. "Bring Della and Ana?"

"AUNTIE LOU ANN wants to see you today." I brought peanut butter toast to the table for the kids' breakfast the following morning. Amazingly, we'd all slept through the night. Ana clutched the blanket she carried everywhere in the house and pulled it over her face.

"How is she?" Della asked. The ceiling fan above us circled softly, barely moving the hot, sticky air.

"Really sick, and even more thin." The words seemed to stick in my throat.

"We're taking you there so you can say goodbye," Mindy said. "It's important to see her one last time."

After breakfast we piled into the car. Mindy held my hand during the entire ten-minute drive. "I'm scared," Ana said as soon as the car stopped.

Mindy turned around and looked at Ana. "Auntie Lou Ann is sick, but she's exactly the same person as always. I'll hold your hand and stay close to you, honey." Mindy opened the car door for the kids, and Ana jumped out and grabbed her hand. Della lagged behind, hands in pockets, feet dragging.

As the four of us walked into Lou Ann's room, I could see the effort it took for her to smile. She'd adjusted the bed so she was sitting up, wrapped a multicolored scarf on her bald head, and pulled the covers up to cover most of her flannel nightgown.

We all walked over to her bed. "Ana, did you have fun at the beach?" Ana nodded her head, but her body stayed stiff. We'd asked the kids to bring Lou Ann a gift.

Ana pulled a folded sheet of paper from her pocket and opened it. "I made this for you." She handed it to Lou Ann. "It's pink hearts."

Lou Ann took the paper. "It's beautiful, Ana. Thank you so much." Her eyes glazed over briefly. She put the drawing on her lap.

Ana's lips and chin trembled. "Bye, Auntie Lou Ann."

"Bye sweetie. I love you." Lou Ann's eyes followed Ana, still clinging to Mindy's hand as she left the room.

As the smile slipped from Lou Ann's face, silent sobs wracked my body. My twin was the one person who constantly pointed out the unique and special qualities of both children. She played games with them, and taught them to make pasta from scratch, build pots, and eat tofu drenched in garlic and fish sauce. I grieved for the loss they were too young to know. Lou Ann turned to nine-year-old Della. "I love you too, Della. So much."

Della walked to the bed and handed Lou Ann a baggy. "Here are some shells for you from the beach in France."

"I really wanted shells." My sister put the baggy on her lap next to the hearts.

Della leaned over and kissed Lou Ann's forehead. "Bye, Auntie Lou Ann."

As Della walked out, the sun dimmed, and the room became painfully quiet.

"How are you?" I asked Lou Ann, grabbing a tissue to wipe my face.

"I'd be crying right now if I could." Her mouth drooped. "Don't let them forget me."

"Never." I still felt drained from the trip, and even more from the good-bye. I sank into the green chair where I'd sat so many times in the weeks and months before, chatting with my sister, doing whatever I could to help. I closed my eyes. Soon Mindy came in to tell me she was taking the kids home. A few minutes passed in silence.

"Ice chips, please," Lou Ann said. I sat forward and spooned a couple of pieces into her open mouth. She motioned me closer and whispered, "I got nine years more than Mom. That's something."

"But I want you to have twenty-nine more years." My heart started to pound. "Growing up, I was the sick twin, and you were the one with the center. Why you, now?"

Lou Ann's face crumpled, but her eyes were dry. "You have the kids . . ."

"And I want *you* to see them grow up."

Lou Ann closed her eyes. "I'm done fighting. Besides, Mom's waiting for me. I feel her close all the time." She paused. "Even closer since that dream. I'm in awe of her love for me." As I settled back into the green chair, I heard her whisper, "She suffered too, you know."

I would replay this moment for years to come. How could Lou Ann slip back and forth between life and death so easily? And how did she feel Mom's love, something I rarely felt while Mom lived? Was forgiveness something that came to everyone with impending death, or was it special to her? How was she able to be so conscious, even as her life force faded away?

Then, in a flash, I knew the answer. My twin, the alchemist, was back. Even as she went about dying, Lou Ann made magic.

32

A Monarch Chrysalis

"You need to take the medication as the doctor prescribed every four hours." I heard the anger in my voice, but I didn't try to hide it. "Pain needs regular medication. If you skip a dose, it doesn't work."

Lou Ann had been refusing her morphine, and Elizabeth asked me to intervene. After a horrific car accident when Della was eight weeks old, I'd spent a pain-filled week in the hospital. Sent home with a prescription for Percocet and strict instructions to swallow two pills every four hours, no matter how drowsy or woozy I felt, I had learned it was the only way to stay in front of the pain, as the nurse told me. Didn't Lou Ann know these things?

"The pain comes and goes," she said. "I'll tell you if I want morphine." The stubborn set to her jaw was more prominent than ever.

We had so little time left I couldn't fight, so I said, "Okay, your choice."

The day before, I'd called Dad to tell him about Lou Ann choosing hospice. He and Henrietta were downstairs now, sitting on Lou Ann's leather sofa and talking with Elizabeth. A couple hours later the bell rang, and Mark and his wife, Cari, walked in. Even though I knew Dad had called him, I wondered if he would make the trip to say goodbye to Lou Ann. Talking about family, particularly Mom, was a frequent topic for Lou Ann and me, but whenever we included our brother, he changed the subject. Over time our visits became less frequent, until we only saw Mark at larger family gatherings. Today he wore dark blue jeans and a short-sleeved flannel shirt, and his close-cropped hair and beard were sprinkled with gray. We were seven years apart, and I hadn't talked with him in the five months since I'd told him about Lou Ann's diagnosis.

I got up to hug him. "So glad you came . . ." I began, my arms out-stretched, but he glanced past me and walked over to Dad.

Dad and Mark slapped each other on the back. "How was the drive?" Dad asked. After Mom died, Dad focused all his energy on ten-year-old Mark, and I knew they talked on the phone every Sunday. Catching myself mid-stride, I turned to hug Cari instead.

She hugged me back. "Here's Mark's famous walnut-wheat bread," she said, handing me a foil-wrapped package. "Baked fresh this morning."

"Let's have some." I led her into the kitchen where the care team, a small group of Lou Ann's closest friends, was eating lunch. I introduced Cari, and we ate toast and caught up. Mark, with Dad on his heels, headed upstairs to Lou Ann's bedroom.

Twenty minutes later, I went upstairs. Mark and Dad were seated across from each other on either side of Lou Ann's bed, deep in conversation. "And the new house?" Dad asked. "What's happening?"

"We got the entire 2,200 feet framed and roofed." Mark leaned back in his chair, lifting the front legs off the floor. "It looks great."

I walked between them and stood by Lou Ann's bed. "Need anything?" I asked in a loud voice, noticing her ice chips were all melted. She nodded at the ice bucket.

When I returned, Mark and Dad were still engrossed in conversation. Lou Ann pushed the button to raise her bed, and as the motor hummed, they talked louder. Lou Ann focused on me as I helped her eat some crushed ice.

A bit later, Mark looked at his watch. "Time to head home."

Dad stood up too. "I'll walk you down."

I waited until I couldn't hear their voices. "Did Mark say goodbye?"

"No, but maybe . . ." She licked her dry lips. "I don't know . . ." She closed her eyes. "I'll sleep now."

Mark stood waiting for me at the bottom of the stairs. "We have to go." He stepped closer and lowered his voice. "I'm not sleeping much. So many bad memories."

After Mark's visit Lou Ann said no more visitors and no unnecessary conversation. Out of necessity, one of us would stay with her, but at her request we sat out of sight and only responded to her needs. Because of that change, Lou Ann never saw the small glass container with a monarch chrysalis a friend had left downstairs on a counter in her kitchen.

Ana and Della loved the book *The Very Hungry Caterpillar*. Our version of the book had soft fabric fruit to touch and real holes in the cardboard leaves where the caterpillar had feasted. Caterpillars emerge ravenous from their birth, eating constantly until they begin their transformation. Lou Ann, too, was ravenous, but only for things of the spirit after cancer took away her pleasure in eating.

Watching her taught me that death was not something to be feared, but something exciting. Her once-active body seemed a hindrance, a shell, except it housed something extraordinary: her growing spirit. During her last days, her eyes were so clear, the blue of them like a sunlit ocean and the whites like a clean bed of snow.

33

A Heart-Shaped Rose Quartz

The following morning, Mindy showed me a posting on CaringBridge from Elizabeth. Lou Ann was nearing the end, and Elizabeth invited us all to the house to hold a vigil. When I arrived, I had to park a block away.

"I have an announcement." Elizabeth spoke over the twenty or so people gathered in their living room. "Lou Ann doesn't have the strength to see anyone, but she wants each of you to have one of her pots." The room became very quiet. "One only please, since more people will be coming by all day." She leaned toward me. "Lou Ann wants you to have two."

I was stunned that she would part with her precious creations—and that she wouldn't tell me in advance. Pushing my way in, I grabbed a small raku pot with a shiny glazed heart on top, a longtime favorite, and a multicolored brown tea pot. Then I hid them in a safe spot. Later, I decided, I'd ask her for two more as keepsakes for Della and Ana.

When it was time for my shift, I positioned myself out of Lou Ann's sight line. Harp music played softly on the boom box, and the room was lit by one small floor lamp by the wall. Just as I got settled, Lou Ann moaned. "My mouth is so dry."

"I'll get you something." I took a small pink sponge on a white plastic stick into the bathroom and held it under cold water. "Try sucking on this." I put the sponge on her tongue.

She grimaced and took it right out. "That's what I call a last resort," she whispered. I watched a trace of a smile flicker on her face; my sister who loved cooking and eating was still in there somewhere. She pointed to her dresser. "I want you to have the rose quartz."

I found the thin, smooth stone shaped like a heart. It was a deep pink color with striations of gray. I put it in my hand where it fit perfectly, and felt warmth radiate from the stone. I still wanted pots for Della and Ana, but when I held the quartz, I was certain I would get them.

"You in pain?" I checked her morphine schedule. "It's past time for your dose."

"I had pain, but it's gone." She looked at me, her face relaxed, eyes clear. "I'll pass on the morphine, but pour me some water." She sighed. "Morphine makes me sleepy, and I don't want to miss anything." She pushed the button to lift the head of the bed and drank a little.

"What would you miss?"

"Hard to explain. Mostly I go to a place where I'm inside this golden light. The music there is different, beyond beautiful." She returned the water glass. "All my pain goes away when I'm there."

I remembered my long-ago dream about flying with the planets, filled with magical light and sound. Could we share a connection to that same place? We sat in silence for a bit until her breathing came fast and harsh. I walked to the bed. "What's wrong?"

"What if I can feel myself dying? Or I'm awake when my heart stops beating?" The air in the room stilled.

"Can't happen. Consciousness always leaves the body first."

"How do you know?" Her eyes opened wide.

"Remember long ago, I told you about remembering past lives where I watched myself die? There was only light and joy, no pain." I squeezed her hand. "I'm sure of that." Lou Ann squeezed back and closed her eyes.

Nothing had changed by evening, so I gathered my two pots and the rose quartz and decided to sleep at home in my own bed. I knew she could go anytime, but I had the sense that I would get a sign, as I had in France, and I'd be at her side.

High, wispy clouds turned the western sky pink as I walked to my car. A few blocks from her house I pulled into the overlook next to Indian Mounds Park to watch the sunset. In the valley below the bluff, the Mississippi River shimmered like a silver ribbon. A small airplane taxied down the runway of the airport far below, lifting gracefully into the air. I watched it until it disappeared.

34

The Orangina Party

"Lou Ann rallied last night." Elizabeth was smiling when I walked in the next morning. We'd had our differences, as most in-laws do, but she had taken such good care of Lou Ann these past months, and I was deeply grateful. "She ate a bit, and we had a little party."

I stumbled on the rug and caught myself. "You had a party?"

"I wish you would have stayed." Karen, part of the care team, looked up from her bowl of cereal. "That flower liqueur you brought from France was superb." Her eyes were moist. "Lou Ann even had some on the sponge." Certainly the rule about no visitors had changed. "Is she up?" I walked toward her room.

"She is." Elizabeth nodded, not meeting my eyes. "She asked for you."

As I walked into the bedroom, Lou Ann sat up in her bed and smiled. Here was the smile I wanted when I got home from France.

"Nice to see you so energetic," I said. Tears pressed behind my eyes.

"I know," she smiled again, wider. "And I'm craving Orangina. Can you get me some?"

Her voice sounded strong, like her old self. The soft rumble of a lawn-mower came through the open window, followed by the smell of freshly cut grass. I leaned over and kissed her cheek.

"I just got here, but I'll go to the store if you want."

"No, stay. I'll ask Pat to go." Lou Ann motioned Pat, another member of the care team, to come in. "Can you get me something else to drink until she gets back?"

I walked downstairs, brightness filling my heart. Maybe I hadn't missed everything. I found a bottle of sarsaparilla root beer, some ice, and a clean glass. As I twisted the top off the bottle, I remembered the hospice nurse saying that as a person readies for death, they crave one last spurt of life, often requesting a favorite food or drink.

Upstairs I heard Lou Ann telling Pat the location of the store and where to find the Orangina with the usual clarity in her voice. I couldn't remember the last time I heard her talk this much.

"I brought you a drink." I held the glass of root beer near her head. She turned and sipped from the bendy straw, smiling. "Tastes like a root beer float," she said.

One beastly hot summer night when we were four, Mom woke us up so we could sit in the kitchen with her and Dad and all have root beer floats. I'd felt so grown-up and happy being awake in the dark night, sipping something sweet with my parents. Since then, Lou Ann and I had often made ourselves root beer floats on special occasions.

Karen was pouring warm lavender oil into her palms. She began to rub Lou Ann's feet. My sister's face relaxed even more as she described the small party last night, how much she enjoyed the Génépi liqueur and her wonderful sleep afterward. I soaked in every detail, imagining the taste of flowers on my tongue. Soon Pat returned with big glass bottles of Orangina, and someone brought long-stemmed wine glasses upstairs. We filled them with ice and the bubbly orange drink. Ice cubes tinkled in our glasses as we clicked them together.

"Here, here!" Lou Ann said, raising her glass. I tried to imagine what she would toast. "To Orangina," she added. I stepped close and clinked my glass against hers. For a moment the sound of ringing glasses filled the room.

After four sips she waved the glass away. "Perfect." She let out a long-satisfied sigh. Pat gathered the glasses and walked downstairs followed by the others. Lou Ann and I were alone again.

"Come lie next to me." Lou Ann patted the narrow space on the bed. I squeezed in on my side next to her. The sheets were soft and cool and smelled faintly of the lavender oil Karen had used on my sister's feet. I slid my arm under her head and cuddled up as close as I could get. As we breathed together, I sank into our connection, our hearts beating in unison. She shifted her body until she faced me. Our noses were practically touching.

"Promise me you'll be okay," she paused, "after I'm gone." Her clear blue eyes held mine without a blink. "Mindy and the kids will keep you here, right?"

A lump rose in my throat. "Don't worry about me," I lied. "I'll be fine."

"First Mom, now me." She sighed. "I'm so sorry to leave you, sis."

My shoulder started to throb, and as I shifted to ease it, Lou Ann began to cough. Our moment was over. I climbed slowly out of the bed, knowing it would probably be our last time.

"I think I'll go home," she murmured.

Her voice was so low I almost missed what she said. Go home. I knew what that meant. Go home to whatever waited for her. Tears started down my cheeks. I sat in the green chair, my favorite, letting the sobs come, letting myself feel the reality of what was happening.

When my sobbing finally eased, I opened my eyes. Lou Ann had fallen asleep. I walked to the bathroom and washed my face, holding the cold washcloth to my burning skin. When I returned, I could see something had shifted. Her eyes were partly open but glazed and unseeing, her breathing shallow. She had entered the final coma. She'd live a few more hours, a day at most, so I decided to sleep there, close by. I called Mindy to let her know.

"Call me the minute anything changes," she said. "My mom is here for the kids so I can be there for you."

I thanked her, then called my folks.

Dinner was a subdued affair, all of Lou Ann's care team only going through the motions of eating. Being together, knowing how much everyone loved my sister, and understanding the sacrifices they'd chosen to make comforted me. We made an overnight schedule, and people spread out to sleep on couches and camping pads. I was on third shift so I went into the spare room. I knew sleep would be hard to come by that night.

"Time to get up." Karen tapped my shoulder. I stumbled into the bathroom where the minty toothpaste and cold water were shocking, but they woke me up. Someone had moved Lou Ann's table lamp onto the floor, and it made a low, soothing circle of golden light. Elizabeth slept deeply, a few feet away from Lou Ann, alone on the bed they used to share. I carried the green chair next to my sister and settled in.

Only a little life remained in her ravaged body. I'd never seen anyone so literally skin and bones. The contour of each blood vessel and cartilage stood out on her face and neck. Blood pulsed through a puffy vein on her forehead in a steady, even beat. The few remaining hairs on her head were white, sparse, and brittle.

Looking at her made my body hurt.

All our lives, people had mistaken me for Lou Ann. My identity was completely intertwined with hers. "You even talk alike," people told us in college. When we both became professionals, they'd add, "How lovely that you're both in helping professions." Purposely, I wore my hair different, got glasses instead of contacts, and dressed differently, but people saw the twin they knew. Soon that would never happen again.

Then who would I be?

Elizabeth thrashed on the nearby bed and I opened my eyes. It was 7:30 a.m. and I'd fallen asleep. As I woke up, Lou Ann's breathing reminded me of the ocean, the rumbling roar of waves going in and out.

35

This Storm's for You

Breakfast was over. The somber care team sat around the kitchen table, mostly silent, waiting. When we heard the rapid footsteps on the stairs and saw Judith peer around the door frame, I knew.

"It's time," she said.

I'd been preparing for this moment for months, but I still felt the shock of it ripple across my skin as I set my glass on the table and went upstairs. We crowded around Lou Ann's bed—her care team, Mindy, Dad, and Henrietta. I heard them breathing behind me as I walked toward the bed.

Lou Ann's gasps for air were more erratic now. Her mouth hung open, her body was still. As I took hold of her icy hand, our intimate moment yesterday seemed years in the past. I wished I could curl around her again and share my warmth, my regular breathing, my life.

"Her hand is so cold." I heard the voice, and I knew I must have spoken out loud because someone responded.

"The blood moves away from the limbs to protect the heart."

I put my hand over her heart, surprised to feel a strong and steady beat even as her breathing grew more labored. The room was lit by the single lamp set on the floor, and the air was sullen with an approaching storm. I could see the sky, a bruised, blue-black color, and I could hear thunder in the distance. My sister's leg jerked twice, and a spasm moved through her arm, as if her spirit was shaking free from her body.

Patrick, dear friend and colleague, leaned forward and placed his large hands on her frail shoulders. "Go home, Lou Ann." His voice was deep and reverent.

The jerking stopped.

"Go on, sweetie," Elizabeth whispered. "I'll survive."

Blasts of wind were battering the house now, stirring a deep memory. Years ago, while backpacking in Glacier National Park, my twin and I had taken shelter under a narrow overhang, screaming with delight as rain poured down from above and hail streamed up within inches of our faces. I remembered Lou Ann's joy at the intensity of the storm, her complete lack of fear. She'd always been that way, confident and courageous. I wondered if the storm outside was welcoming her in some way.

So I leaned over and whispered in her ear, "This storm's for you, sis. To take you home."

She must have heard me, because her breathing stopped for three heart-beats and started again. Riveted, I watched her ribs rise and fall, the raspy sounds of her breath a counterpoint to the steady pulse of energy under my hand.

"I'll always remember you." My eyes burned as tears dripped from my chin. "Go in peace."

Wind lashed a tree branch against the bedroom window, and rain began to pound the roof, sliding off in sheets. Light and shadow flickered across Lou Ann's face followed by the sound of a loud crack as the lights went off. The air conditioner growled, shuddered, and stopped. Someone behind me opened a window, and the fresh, earthy smells of rain filled the room.

Lou Ann inhaled, exhaled, and paused. Her rib cage rose and fell. Rain blew across her bed, and onto my face. Exhilaration, ecstasy, and fury coursed through me. My sister's heart beat faster and faster. It rocketed against my hand three times, then nothing.

The time was 1:05 p.m., July 23, 2005.

Never before had my heart felt so full or so broken. I knew my life would never be the same. Ever.

"She's gone," I said.

Our friend Karen moved to close Lou Ann's eyes. I'd never seen anyone do this except on TV. Gently, she put two fingers on Lou Ann's eyelids and pulled them down. Her eyes moved back to half-mast. Karen tried again. Again, they returned.

"She always was real stubborn," Dad said. Laughter filled the room for a moment, immediately followed by harsh sobbing.

I heard thunder murmur in the distance as the storm receded. A layer of whiteness spread across Lou Ann's face as her cheeks collapsed inward and her body stiffened. A vise closed around my heart. Time stopped. A vast force pulled at my feet, and I longed to meld into her, seeing my own body lying there too, until Mindy's safe arms cradled me, her voice soft in my ear, and I could breathe again.

Part Three
The Solo Path

**

it was when i stopped searching for home within others and lifted the foundations of home within myself i found there were no roots more intimate than those between a mind and body that have decided to be whole.

—RUPI KAUR

36
A Caring Community

The ceiling fan in our living room whooshed around hypnotically. I lay on the couch, trying to rest. I couldn't remember how I'd gotten home. Mindy's voice floated down the stairs, and I knew she'd gone to tell the kids about Lou Ann. Their muffled sobs weighed heavy on my heart.

There was a knock at the back door, and I pushed myself up. Our friends Susan and Judy stood outside, holding covered platters of food. "We brought veggies, tabouli, pita, and hummus," they said.

"I'll put them on the table." In true shiva tradition they'd begun the week of community involvement, caring for the mourners. By seven that evening, more family and friends crowded into our small downstairs, and the dining room table was covered with food. After greetings they gathered in small groups, talking and crying in hushed tones.

Elizabeth arrived a bit later with the care team who'd stayed behind to prepare Lou Ann for cremation the next day. Her eyes were red and glazed. She took my hand. "I planned a little ceremony," she said. "Please come."

Elizabeth and I had had our ups and downs; we'd gotten along because of our family relationship, and during Lou Ann's illness, I'd seen her compassion and deep caring for my sister. But the thought of Lou Ann becoming ashes rent me apart inside. For a moment, I could barely breathe.

"I can't."

Elizabeth nodded. I hoped she understood.

Mindy had joined me on the couch. I was still wearing the wrinkled T-shirt and shorts I'd slept in at my sister's. I felt clammy and smelled sour, but there was no time to change. "Mindy," I asked her, "have you seen Dad?"

She took my hand. "Didn't he tell you?"

"I talked with Henrietta . . ."

"They aren't coming."

Typical, I thought. Instinctively, I looked around for Lou Ann so we could joke about how Dad was being Dad. But Lou Ann and I would never joke, laugh, or cry together again. I buried my face in Mindy's neck.

At last, the rabbi walked in the door and it was time to begin. Someone handed out small stapled booklets of prayers as the house quieted. I leaned deeper into Mindy, holding her hand like a lifeline. The rabbi, draped in her white prayer shawl, began to chant. She recited a few prayers followed by a responsive reading. I followed the words in the book but said nothing. What was I doing here? Where was my sister? Memories of the loneliness, depression, and isolation that haunted me after Mom's death clogged my throat.

The rabbi gestured to the group. "Will everyone please rise for the mourner's kaddish?"

As I stood, my legs began to shake. Mindy stepped closer, her arm strong around my waist. Deep voices joined with higher ones, soft intonations with loud ones, mixing into one voice reciting the prayer. In the words I heard love for my sister, grief and sadness for her death, and caring and compassion for my family. The chanting enveloped my sobs as Mindy held me tight.

Afterward, people came up, took my hand, and spoke to me of their sorrow and love for Lou Ann. Many promised to return during the next seven days. By the time everyone left, the food had been stored, the couches and chairs were back in place, and the kitchen was clean. Upstairs I heard the kids' high animated voices calling, "Look, Grandma," and, "This book, Grandma." What a gift to have Mindy's mother here.

"How'd you like the service?" I said out loud to Lou Ann. "A great turn-out, huh?" My eyes burned. "I missed you." I'd never felt this alone. We'd lived on different continents, been out of phone contact, had fights where we didn't speak for full weeks, but nothing had felt like this disconnect, this emptiness. I had no idea how to make it better, or if it would ever change.

The seven days of shiva ran into each other with people at the house from morning until dusk. A friend brought her guitar and led us in song, another brought her children and took Della and Ana to the park, and clients of mine came to offer me support. Even one of Della's teachers came. People who knew Lou Ann shared memories of her, and everyone brought food. At mealtimes I watched Della and Ana filling their plates and relaxed for a moment in the comfort, care, and love around me. This was what shiva was meant to be.

On the last day, as the bright summer sun glared against the kitchen windows, Mindy handed me the cordless phone, saying it was Aunt Dianne. I walked into the small downstairs bathroom for privacy and sat on the hard plastic toilet seat.

"Oh honey, I can't even imagine what you're going through." Dianne's strong voice belied her eighty years. The kindness in her voice triggered a memory. "You go ahead and cry," she had told us after Mom died. "What happened is a terrible tragedy, and don't let your father pretend otherwise."

I choked through a sob, "I miss Lou Ann so much."

"Of course you do," she said. "I want to tell you something, Linda." She paused. "You know I lost my husband, your uncle, twenty years ago and then my daughter two years later, both of them to cancer." I shifted my weight on the closed toilet. "Those were both unbearable, but I had my twin and she got me through." I heard a catch in her voice. "It's the worst thing I can imagine, losing your twin. It's like part of you dying."

31

Death Chart

Once shiva ended there was no reason to get out of bed and my bed turned into an ocean of pain. I was tossed and churned, smashed by grief; the shore distant, too far to reach. Tears burned my eyes, my throat was scrubbed raw from sobs. Inside, I felt hollow, an empty vessel pummeled by onslaught after onslaught of grief, leaving me battered and forlorn. I'd always been a twin. Part of something bigger. A unit. Lou Ann had always been there, and I counted on her. She was the only one who understood me completely.

A lawn mower hummed outside my bedroom window, bringing the smell of freshly cut grass. I remembered running across the lawn in front of our childhood home after my father mowed. An image came of the summer before sixth grade, how my skin smelled of sweat and sunshine as I galloped behind my sister. Her long, coltish legs reminded me of horses prancing as she whinnied, her thick hair glowing golden in the midday sun. Lou Ann would want me to live. Even after she was gone, she'd want me to carry on without her. I had promised her I would when I told her to go home.

I sat up, forcing myself out of bed. I walked into the hall and down the carpeted steps, listening for footsteps or voices, anything. The house was utterly silent. Even the cats slept, curled together on the couch.

I noticed the cardboard box of childhood photos. I slowly spread them on the dining room table, taking my time with each one. Some were old, with scalloped edges, tiny black and whites. Some were more recent, full color. Some had faded. Here we were, at all different ages, so alike that people couldn't tell us apart. In our baby pictures I didn't know who was who. Deep in the box, I found the one video I had of Lou Ann, a recording of fifteen minutes when she shared her lunch with sixteen-month-old Ana. I slid it into our VCR and watched her smile at me from the screen. Where was she? My heart felt blank. Where was the connection I had been sure would happen after her death? We were twins, after all; she wouldn't really leave me. I had my skill of knowing things before they happened, and my prophetic dreams, but she hadn't shown up in either yet. And the pictures made me miss her more. I decided to walk the mile to my new office. A few weeks earlier I'd moved her office furniture there, arranging it in a beautiful way, surprised by how much pleasure it gave me. Maybe being close to her possessions would help.

As I arrived, I heard voices from the nearby massage-therapy studio. The sign on the door read "Psychic Massage by Joan." Moments later I heard Joan's client leave, so I went over and knocked lightly. A voice invited me inside. Joan wore a purple sweater, and her wavy gray hair rested on her shoulders. We hadn't met yet, so I stood in the doorway and introduced myself. As I walked in, the door slipped out of my hand, and I had to turn around to close it.

"Someone walked in behind you," Joan said. A distinctive raku teapot sat on a shelf next to her.

"Was it my twin, Lou Ann? She just died. Can you see her?" My voice climbed higher with each question, as I searched Joan's face for a sign.

"I can't help you," she shook her head. "You need more time to heal."

"But I need to talk to her." Tears ran down my cheeks. "I'll make an appointment."

"It was nice to meet you, Linda." She gave me a sad smile and turned back to her desk.

I stumbled down the hall to my office and found my keys. Closing the door behind me, I collapsed into Lou Ann's wingback chair. Why was Joan, a stranger, able to see Lou Ann when I couldn't? I lifted a raku pot from a nearby table and ran my fingers over the smooth sides, hoping to feel her creative energy. Nothing.

I angrily swiped at my wet face and pushed myself to my feet, shuffling through a pile of papers on my desk. There it was, her death chart. I'd created it a month ago and studied it occasionally since then, trying to understand her moment of death. I needed answers.

I clicked on a light and sank into my desk chair. The chart was computer-generated, full of symbols and lines that meant everything to me and little to anyone who didn't know astrology. Making it had taken me two minutes, but the journey to understanding it would take a long time.

Right off, I saw Chiron, the wounded healer archetype, on the soul point, or nadir, of Lou Ann's death chart. I thought about that day at the lake when she shared her longing to be a mom, how that was one of her few regrets. Regrets were all about wounds, what a person had not brought into her life, what she missed with a deep ache in the soul. Chiron was situated at the point of Lou Ann's deepest longings, origins and family. I knew how much I'd gained from being a parent. Raising my kids forced me to face Mom's abuse, something Lou Ann and I had never agreed on. I thought I knew why: Lou Ann had been the favored child and I the jealous one on the sidelines of our mother's love. I wondered again if my jealousy of my sister had been misguided—it seemed parental approval mattered little when compared to things. Like death.

Staring at Chiron on Lou Ann's death chart made me realize something else. It was opposite the sun, Saturn conjunction, a profound symbol for the end of a person's life force. If I had been the ill twin, if I hadn't had my children to keep me here, death might have seemed appealing. I sat back in the chair, my finger still tracing symbols on the chart. Clearly Joan the psychic had done me a favor by not responding to my desperate questions. I needed to discover answers for myself.

38

Too Late

I tapped my foot and waited as Ana and Della ran upstairs one more time to get something they'd forgotten. My sweaty fingers stuck to the manila envelope in my hand. Inside were photos carefully chosen for the memorial tables and the eulogy. Photos that represented the beauty and courage of my sister, so that everyone could see her as she lived. Mindy had helped me, and I was pleased with it, having spent hours on the selection. I couldn't bring my sister to the memorial service, but I could celebrate her.

The kids clattered down the stairs, and we filed out to the car. Everyone was utterly silent on the ride to our old childhood synagogue, now a Unitarian Universalist Church. We'd chosen the church for the service because of their acceptance of LGBT people and because of its history with our family.

The front entryway hadn't changed in the last thirty years. It still smelled faintly of floor wax. Mindy and the kids walked up to the sanctuary while I went into the social hall to arrange the photos. The room was quiet and dim, the overhead fluorescents were off, and only three high windows on one wall let in light. Tables and chairs were set up for the reception, and around the edge of the room were the photo albums and boards Elizabeth had arranged.

We'd talked earlier about the service, reception, and photos, agreeing there would be no intimate photos of Lou Ann. Just good memories, we'd promised each other. The pictures drew me like a magnetic beam: In a patchwork of glossy rectangles, Lou Ann enjoyed many wilderness adventures; in one she stood by a tall pine tree with her large brown pack at her feet and a big smile on her face, silhouetted by a range of snow-capped mountains. In another, she perched on a log next to a bright campfire, holding a cooking pot, and in yet another she and Elizabeth paddled a canoe through churning rapids. A tiny flutter of happiness tickled my breastbone when I thought about how much my sister had enjoyed life.

I opened my envelope and arranged the baby pictures I'd brought, the photos of our middle years and beyond, my favorite ones of Lou Ann with Della and Ana. I stood back, satisfied. The photos were a fitting tribute.

I could hear conversations from the hall. More people were arriving, greeting each other in subdued voices. I wanted to join them, but I hadn't yet looked at the final table. I walked over slowly, tucking my empty envelope into my bag. These photos were not arranged in a pleasing display. Instead, Elizabeth had erected a tall, white photo board and filled it with oversized pictures of Lou Ann from her last days, her face gaunt, her eyes hollow and staring into the distance, her death so close.

Pressure built behind my eyes. I imagined slamming the boards down, ripping off the photos and throwing them in the trash. I turned away from the outrage, frantically looking for Mindy, but she and the kids were already inside. I saw Judith walking down the hall and marched over to her.

"Did you see that photo board?" I struggled to control my voice. "The dying photos?"

Judith gave me a sad smile. "I don't like them either," she said, "But Lou Ann's clients need to know she didn't choose to leave."

"Choose to leave!" I sputtered. I took a shaky breath. "She would hate people seeing her that way." *I hate seeing her that way*, I thought.

Judith put a hand on my shoulder, and I fought not to shake it off. "I know," she said. "But it's too late to change it." It was. It was too late for a lot of things. I felt the fight drain from my body.

"The service is about to start." Judith gave my shoulder a little squeeze. "Go sit with your family."

I made my feet move down the long aisle to the front row of the sanctuary, where Mindy sat with Della and Ana. I settled in, tuning out the low hum of voices around me. This had been our spiritual home for many years before Mom's death. Lou Ann and I attended Hebrew School and celebrated our b'nai mitzvah here. Every week for over ten years, we learned about Judaism, sang Sabbath prayers, and celebrated holidays. The entire building reminded me of my twin. Elizabeth had been right to suggest we hold the memorial here, even though my spirituality had grown beyond religion. It lived in my loving of the heavens; studying astrology and helping my clients; and trusting my inner knowing, my dreams, and the beauty of nature and wilderness.

Gradually the room quieted. "Please stand for the mourner's kaddish," the rabbi said. "*Yitgadal v'yitkadash sh'mei raba . . .*" The familiar words reminded me of Mom's death, and tears coursed down my cheeks. Almost forty years ago, Lou Ann and I had stood in this very room, singled out by our mother's death, reciting this prayer. Mindy's arm came around my shoulders, holding me tight. "*B'alma di v'rachirutei . . .*" On the other side Della leaned into me. Then Ana squeezed in front of me, resting her head on my midriff. My tears poured out, wetting Ana's hair.

As the prayer quieted, our friend Janet walked to the microphone. She reminisced about the spiritual side of my sister's life, their long conversations about religion and philosophy, and more recently about illness and death. I heard quiet cries and people blowing their noses around me.

Then Patrick walked to the podium. The light reflected off his round glasses as he shifted his weight from foot to foot. "Lou Ann and I had lunch together without fail once a month for seventeen years." The room was completely silent. He stopped talking and covered his face with his hand as his body shook with sobs. "And most often what we talked about was work. Lou Ann was completely devoted to her clients. She was happiest helping people." He took a deep breath. "Her death is a terrible loss for us all."

A woman half rose in her seat, turning to face the congregation. "Lou Ann was my therapist, and when I started seeing her I was in a deep depression, suicidal in fact." She sobbed for a moment, like Patrick had. "I owe her my life."

Finally it was my turn. I squeezed Mindy's hand for courage and walked to the microphone. "At first I tried to write a eulogy that was just about Lou Ann since it is her life we're commemorating today. Then I realized that was impossible." I kept my eyes glued on my notes. If I started crying I wouldn't be able to stop, so I swallowed my tears. "Even though we were two separate people, in many ways we were one." I heard murmurs of agreement.

"As preschoolers we loved to play little mommy and little daddy. Somehow Lou Ann always managed to be little daddy and leave me with all the housework." The sound of soft laughter moved like a wave from the back of the room. When I looked up, Mindy nodded encouragement, and the knot in my stomach started to dissolve.

"During grade school we loved pretending to be horses and spent hours working on perfecting our ability to trot and canter." I paused for a moment, remembering Lou Ann in the front yard of our Oliver Avenue house. Her long blond-brown hair blew behind her as she sped across the yard, whinnying with abandon. A pain tore at my heart. "Lou Ann was a really good horse," I said, and people chuckled again.

Choosing the right anecdotes before the service had felt almost as impossible as gathering the photos. I needed ones that would honor my sister and share her vitality and spirit. Before I spoke my final words, I looked around the sanctuary, uncertain if my brother Mark had come at all, but there he sat between his wife and Dad. So I talked about Lou Ann's and my exclusive relationship as twins, how it could sometimes keep others away. I saw my brother nod; his face softened and something inside me did too. After the service I looked for him in the reception hall but couldn't find him.

At the reception, people crowded around with condolences. A blond woman was speaking to me about Lou Ann being a rising star in the psychoanalytic community, not just here, but nationally. I felt my composure about to break. I raced down the long familiar hall to the bathroom. How could my twin be such a rising star, saving lives, and then be taken so soon? I'd always seen us growing old together, her continuing to love and teach my children, and help so many more clients. I tore at the paper towel dispenser, unleashing a cascade of towels. Her death chart still made sense, but I didn't care about Chiron. I wanted her back.

I slammed the stall door, crouching on the toilet, my face buried in the soaked wad of paper towels. I heard the bathroom door open.

"Ema, you in here?" It was Della, calling me the Hebrew name for mother.

I blew my nose in the rough paper. "Be out in a sec, honey."

When I opened the stall door, Della stood there, clutching a rolled-up children's activity book. I remembered Lou Ann and me coloring in books like those at that age. "Can I stay here with you?" Tears gathered in Della's eyes. "Too many sad people out there."

I put my arms around my child. "Sweetie, it's fine to cry. That's how we heal." Della leaned against me, shaking with silent sobs. "It's hard to lose someone at age nine, and this is a big loss." Della lifted a tear-streaked face. "I'll always comfort you, even when I'm sad," I said. "No acting strong, OK?"

39

Welcoming the Darkness

The next morning the kids slept late. Mindy and I sat at the dining room table drinking coffee and reading the newspaper. Mindy cleared her throat, and I looked up. "I want to do something fun for your birthday."

How could I celebrate without Lou Ann? I wiped my hands on my jeans. "I'm already getting a massage that day; that seems like plenty of celebration."

"It's still your birthday." Mindy slid her chair over and wrapped me in a long hug. "Let's make it special."

Suddenly sad beyond measure, I could only shrug. Her comforting arm dropped away as I stood up and collected our coffee cups. "You decide," I mumbled. "I don't care."

I SANK INTO the luxury of my birthday massage, wondering what Mindy had arranged. When I got home in the early afternoon, our four closest friends had arrived. I'd been friends with these women long before I met Mindy, drawn together by politics, love of astrology, and the outdoors. Mindy fit in well and quickly. Even our children loved and accepted them as extended family.

At their insistence, I stayed out of the kitchen. I went to our bedroom and pulled out the charts again, thinking about my sister and how we usually celebrated our birthday.

Some years, we'd meet just to exchange gifts. Other times, we'd plan a big bash, renting a hall for a dance party, combining all our friends. They were clear markers in my year, these birthday gatherings, and I felt heavy despite the delicious smells that wafted up from the kitchen below and the clatter of china and silver coming from the dining room.

"Dinner in five." I heard Susan's voice calling up to me from the foot of the stairs, so I gathered myself, wiped my face, and put on my best smile.

I came downstairs slowly, and my friends and family were gathered around a table filled with food and flowers. Della and Ana grinned at me from their chairs.

"Happy Birthday, sweetie," Mindy said, as I took my seat. She leaned over to give me a kiss.

"To a year that can only get better." Susan raised her glass.

As I sipped sparkling cider and nodded my thanks through watering eyes, a small soft voice told me I might not be as alone as I thought.

Mindy went back to work, and both kids returned to school, leaving the house tomb-like. The usually active cats slept curled up together on the couch. Even though I still had nothing to give and had cancelled my clients for a few weeks, I hoped something normal would help me feel better. I decided to drive to my office and pick up mail. Walking to the car, I felt detached from my body, as if I floated slightly above it. Because I remembered feeling like this after Mom died, I told myself it was normal.

On St. Clair Avenue, sunlight reflected off a large glass window, and I squinted my eyes against the sudden brightness. As I focused back on the road, I saw Lou Ann's tan Toyota Corolla in front of me. It had the black and white KFAI radio station bumper sticker next to the small dent on the left back fender. Energy flooded through my body. It had all been a terrible dream; she was alive. I pressed my foot to the accelerator to catch up. The whoosh of the tires against the road, the hum of the air conditioner, and the bright blueness of the sky were sharp in my awareness. As my car pulled alongside the Toyota, I strained to catch a glimpse of my sister. Instead I saw Elizabeth's profile.

She turned left, leaving me behind. I pulled the car over onto the shoulder, slumping over the steering wheel, furious with Elizabeth, with my twin, with the world. What made me think I would see Lou Ann? Now furious at myself, I put the car into gear, made a sloppy U-turn, and headed home. Once inside, I turned off the phone, pulled down the shades, and, welcoming the darkness, dove under the covers.

A few days later we were on the third floor of the Mall of America inside the store Candy-Candy. Both kids filled cellophane bags with a variety of sweets as I inhaled the sugary and fruity smells, glad Mindy had convinced me to go out.

My cell phone rang. When I flipped it open, I saw it was Dad. I'd spoken with my father at Lou Ann's memorial and again a few weeks after that, but the emptiness I felt looking around for him hours after Lou Ann died still hurt. In contrast to Henrietta, who'd called to say she could barely imagine how I'd get along without my twin, he'd never said a word.

"Linda," I could hear the tremor in his voice, "I still can't believe Lou Ann is gone."

"Dad, please stop." I walked over to a slated wooden bench and sat down. "I'm too deep in my own grief." I could feel the familiar pressure behind my eyes.

"Parents aren't supposed to outlive their children, Linda."

I ached with all the times I'd wanted something from my father and been disappointed. Parents were supposed to console their children, not the other way around. I felt a slow burn travel from my belly into my throat. Here was a man who hadn't protected me from Mom's violence or the neighbor's sexual assault, and now he wanted to lean on me.

"I can't help you," I said, "I'm hanging up now." I snapped the phone shut in my shaking hand.

Weeks later, I noticed a grocery-store display of turkeys for Thanksgiving, a few weeks away. By now, Lou Ann and I would be planning menus and deciding whose turn it was to host. Barely making eye contact with the cashier, I grabbed my bag of groceries and ran for the car. No way could I sit through a Thanksgiving dinner with Dad. I told Mindy about my decision as soon as I got home. "They're adults, honey," she said, over the sound of the dishwasher. "It's never too soon to create a new tradition."

Lou Ann's death took so much from my life, but it did launch new traditions. I didn't know that a relaxed intimate gathering of dear friends for Thanksgiving would satisfy me in a way that the larger, more stress-filled family occasion never did. Nor did I know that within the four years following Lou Ann's death, Henrietta would die, followed five months later by my father.

40

Her Own Trajectory

"At least you have a sister!" I screamed at Della and Ana as I tried to intervene in their heated battle. Normally I kept calm and helped them find a way to resolve their problems. My face was hot as I marched upstairs, running from my crying children. I closed all the blinds and pulled up the covers, hiding from them, from myself, from everyone, shaken to the core at what I'd just done. My own mother had leaked out of me when I least expected it.

"What's wrong?" Mindy asked fifteen minutes later as she walked into the bedroom, clicking on a light. We'd purchased that lamp in a small neighborhood shop. It was one of our first purchases after we decided to make a life together, and I loved it. She sat next to me on the bed. "The kids said you yelled at them."

"They were having a small problem." I took a deep breath. "I made it much worse." Mindy took my hand and I scooted closer to her. "I don't know if I can parent them right now."

My life partner sat for a few moments, stroking my hair. We listened to each other's breathing, and I felt my breath calm down, some of the guilt washing away with her kind touch. She had always loved me, even with the legacy I brought from my mom, even through my initial awkwardness while parenting these beloved children of ours, and now I couldn't even control myself.

"It's the grief," I whispered.

"I know," she said. "I found a grief support group for you at a church nearby. Maybe it's time to go."

THE CHURCH WAS easy to find. Only a dozen cars sat in the parking lot, and I hoped the meeting would be small. I followed the signs to a paneled room where about six women and four men, all middle-aged, sat on metal folding chairs. I found a chair in the back row in case I wanted to leave early.

Right at seven o'clock, a tall red-haired woman walked to the front of the room. "Pull your chairs into a circle," she said, "and we'll get started." Chairs scraped against the linoleum floor as everyone moved. She led us through introductions, asking us to say our names, which family member died, and how long ago that happened. As we went around the circle, I realized everyone else was grieving the loss of a parent. Then she opened up the floor for sharing stories, giving each of us ten minutes to talk and ask for support from the group.

How could I possibly get any help in ten minutes? And no one here had lost a sibling, let alone a twin. I longed for my safe spot at the back of the room.

"My mother passed away seven months ago from bladder cancer," a gray-haired woman said, her chin trembling. "We had a difficult relationship, but it's hard to live without her."

"That sounds awful," someone replied. I shifted around on the hard folding chair.

"We miss people even if it was a bad relationship," the leader said.

A man with a long beard jumped in. "Maybe you could find a hobby. Learning guitar has helped me."

Right after her diagnosis, I'd asked Lou Ann if she was interested in an ovarian cancer support group. She declined instantly, explaining that her training made it hard to take part in a bad therapy group. Here I was, sitting in just such a group.

The room had grown quiet. I looked up. Everyone was staring at me, waiting.

"My identical twin sister died in July from cancer," I began. My voice sounded far away. "We were always being mistaken for each other." My cheeks were suddenly wet. "She's not even alive, and people still call me by her name. I don't know how I'm going to live without her."

There was silence after I finished, the weight of my introduction hanging in the room. Then the leader said something and other people began to talk. No one suggested I start a hobby, or if they did, I didn't hear it. My ears were filled with a buzzing sound, and I tried desperately to hear Lou Ann's voice, telling me a story, sharing a joke, whispering something for me alone.

I continued to weep silently. Around me, other people were wiping away tears, immersed in their own pain. As soon as the meeting ended, I gathered my coat and left. There had to be a better way to heal. Mindy was asleep when I got home. As I crawled into bed, I saw the copy of the death chart I'd left on my night table. It was a plain sheet of white paper, the circles and symbols so familiar to me after all my years as an astrologer. I stared at it in the dim light of our bedroom, listening to Mindy breathe, hearing the night noises outside the window. I knew that somehow this chart held the secret of why Lou Ann was gone and why I was still here.

As I stared at the chart, something caught my eye. The moon's nodes are important in all astrological charts, showing where the moon's orbit intersects the path the Earth makes around the sun. At the moment of Lou Ann's death, the moon's south node was rising in Libra. A powerful symbol. It indicated an intense loss of energy, like trying to run a bath with taps full on but the drain open. I thought back to my studies and what I knew about this symbol, and I remembered learning it also symbolized the release of karma that was years- or even lifetimes-old. Its prominence suggested that it was time for Lou Ann to go back to the place of wisdom between death and birth.

I set the chart back on my table and clicked off the light, settling in beside Mindy. From an astrological point of view, Lou Ann's life force certainly had run out, like water going down a drain. I watched it leaking away over her last days, but I'd also felt her deep sense of going home. Her karma being completed had startled and even saddened me at the time, but now I realized she might have been aware that she'd fulfilled her time here.

She was separate from me, on her own trajectory. She seemed to know her life was over, and she'd done what she came to do. What if her knowing this was the most important thing, more important than my emptiness and loss at being left behind?

41

Haunting Nightmares

I slipped the car into park. In front of me hung the big wooden sign: Center for Grief, Loss, and Transition. Mindy had found this therapist, who was highly recommended, she said. And I needed someone. I'd looked at the death chart on nights when I was woken by nightmares that made sleep nearly impossible. I was learning a lot but was still haunted by visions of Lou Ann disappearing down chaotic streets crowded with people and cars. I felt detached from my body, but I'd gotten used to that over the past months since Lou Ann's death.

I mustered a smile, took the forms the receptionist handed me, sat at a small table, and began filling them out. Medical history, psychiatric history, too many details. I had put down my pen after answering the first question, already exhausted, when someone spoke.

"I'm Gayle, and you must be Linda."

A woman in her forties with black shoulder-length hair, a bright smile, and a kind face stood over me. She picked up my incomplete forms and beckoned me to follow her.

Her office was a sky-colored room full of windows, plants, and wicker furniture, but the smell stopped me as I entered. On a low glass table sat a bowl of fragrant cinnamon potpourri. The sweetness permeated the room, and I was immediately transported to a cool fall day in Lou Ann's kitchen when we baked apples pies. Sobs tore through me.

"It's my twin sister. She died five months ago, and I don't know how to live without her."

I looked up. Gayle's eyes were soft. "I'm the mother of eight-year-old twins." She smiled as she said their names. "Their bond is amazing. They're always getting into trouble together and sticking up for each other. They don't do any of that with their older brother."

"Yeah, Lou Ann and I were a team, all right." I wiped my face with some tissues.

"How did Lou Ann die?"

I let out the breath I'd been holding, took off my coat, and settled into one of the comfortable chairs. Gayle sat quietly, waiting. The words came slowly at first, then in a rush. I talked nonstop, relating each detail from the beginning of Lou Ann's illness, including my premonition that she wouldn't recover. I talked about seeing her hair fall out and being reminded of Mom; I described every frustrating visit to the doctor. I hadn't realized how desperately I needed to tell the entire story.

It wasn't that Mindy and my friends didn't hear me, didn't get what I was going through—they did. But they had their own feelings and pain about Lou Ann's death. This stranger, listening to me with her whole being, was neutral. She gave me space, quiet, and understanding without adding any of her own experience into the mix.

The hour passed so quickly that I was surprised when Gayle looked at her watch. "I can't wait to hear more, Linda," she said, rising from her chair, "but we're out of time for today."

After two months of weekly sessions, Gayle suggested I make an appointment with a homeopath. I'd worked with homeopathy before and knew its potential to heal in deep and fast ways. The homeopath also listened to me carefully and then sent me home with two small pills in a glass bottle. As I sat in bed the night after the appointment and turned the bottle up and down, I watched the two round pills move apart, then collide, and I felt strangely comforted by their movement. Then I popped off the cap and placed one under my tongue to dissolve.

The morning after the second dose I awakened with a start. My heart was racing and I hurt all over. As I rolled onto my back in bed, the room around me grew dim and I was transported to a cold, musty funeral hall. Dad and Lou Ann stood next to me, and I heard my brother Mark whimper. Dad took Lou Ann's and Mark's hands, pulling them toward the open coffin where my mother lay, but I stood frozen in place. Then, just as suddenly, I was in Lou Ann's storm-darkened bedroom where her cancer-ravaged body laid motionless on the bed. My ears rang with the sound of Grandma's piercing cries combined with sirens as the coroner approached Lou Ann's house. I opened my eyes and gasped for breath, but the memories didn't stop. My legs were freezing cold as they lowered Mom's casket into the ground; then my face burned as I refused to participate in Lou Ann's cremation. I heard wounded animal sounds and realized they were coming from me. Whitecaps of grief plunged me higher and deeper than before. Hours passed. Exhausted, I fell asleep until the shrill sound of the alarm reminded me to pick up Della and Ana from school.

I navigated the short drive to my children's school and then back home. I dragged myself along as I poured glasses of apple juice and opened a box of graham crackers, hoping they didn't notice my fatigue.

It was hard to sleep that night; I didn't know what I'd wake to. I wanted the return of these inner experiences, a connection to something universal that had both startled and comforted me all of my life. I couldn't figure out where they'd gone since Lou Ann's death, but I didn't expect such a shocking reentry. Eventually, I did fall asleep.

The following morning, I awoke to a bedroom filled with muted light. When I stood, my body felt light and limber, as if I'd let go of a heavy weight I hadn't even been aware of carrying. Shimmering sunlight danced on white snowy branches outside the bedroom windows. A winter bird trilled a song, and a moment later another bird replied. When my stomach rumbled, I realized I hadn't felt hungry in months. As the eggs sizzled in the pan, I made a shopping list for a big stir-fry dinner that night.

Those two tiny pills and the regular meetings with Gayle had worked some astonishing magic.

42

Three Goodbyes

As I drove to my office, I hoped I was ready to return to work. My days had grown too empty and the periods of overwhelming grief felt more intermittent, so when a longtime client left a message saying it was important to meet, I decided to see her. Being in the moment with clients and looking to the stars to help them had a way of centering me, giving me energy and a sense of alignment with something greater. As I walked in the door, I made a wish for that to happen in our session—for both myself and Carol.

"My husband has bladder cancer," Carol said, settling herself on the long green couch as we started our session. Tears leaked down her cheeks, and she dabbed at them with a Kleenex. Two small rivers of mascara followed her tears. "Please tell me how I can be strong, because it upsets him when I cry." I remembered that Carol had married Sam ten years earlier, telling me that finally she'd found the love of her life. "Someone said I'm in my second Saturn Return. Am I?" She tucked the crumpled tissues in her purse.

I put her chart, a round wheel with colorful symbols, on the table between us. "Here is your Saturn." With a bright pink marker I highlighted the position of Saturn that day. "This is how it looks when it returns. It's almost exact."

She leaned forward and peered at the chart. "How often does this happen?"

"Every twenty-nine years. Saturn Returns bring intense life lessons that force people to change priorities, come to terms with harsh realities, and deal with limitations, burdens, and responsibilities." I thought back to my first Saturn Return. My first office burned, I was rejected by my folks for being lesbian, and I'd ended up having emergency surgery. Carol's chart showed an easier road, but still promised months marked by the fear and anxiety she already felt about her husband.

"So how can I be strong?" she asked.

"I don't believe in that." I remembered the powerful sinking feeling in my body when I learned Lou Ann was diagnosed with stage four cancer. The day she called I cried so hard I scared both my children. I knew then, because of what was happening in our charts, that she would die. Through her illness, her death, and my grief, I'd decided against being strong and tears became a regular part of my daily life. "I might be able to tell you how to cope, though. I know that tears release a chemical that helps us heal." This reading was already different than the day Jennifer told me her brother had died. I was in the flow.

"Sam feels like he has to take care of me when I cry. That's why I want to stop." Carol's chin trembled.

"Is that true? Do you need to be taken care of?"

"No," she quietly sobbed. "I can't hold the tears inside." We sat for a moment.

"Tell Sam you can give him what he needs, even if you cry, and that crying helps you cope."

After Carol left, I realized astrology had worked. I sat down at my computer and sent out an email saying I was returning to work. I should have known that now, as I'd done so many other times in my career, I would attract clients who mirrored my life issues.

Tom PLAYED WITH his Twins baseball cap, adjusting it again and again on his head. I'd agreed to fit him in an already busy day after he'd left a dozen messages, each becoming more urgent.

"Tell me why you're here."

He adjusted his cap again. "I got your name from Laura. I have an inoperable brain tumor, and it's just a matter of months before I die." His voice was steady even though the fidgeting continued. "I have a wife and two kids, and I want to know how long I have to get my affairs in order."

A few months had passed since Lou Ann died, and I struggled to push away the familiar pressure behind my eyes. I took a deep breath. "I don't really make predictions about death, but I can tell you about coming cycles."

Tom looked at his hands. "I need help preparing myself and my family." He took off the cap and held it. His bald head reminded me of a sick Lou Ann.

After another deep breath I handed him a copy of his chart. Because he wanted a forecast, there were two concentric wheels on the computer paper. The inner one held symbols reflecting his natal chart, or life potential; the outer one, a chart for the year, showed what was important right now. I handed him a copy but kept one where I'd added a third ring by hand, using colored markers to position the planets in the zodiac for that day. "Please check the three lines below your name to make sure the birthdate, birthplace, and birth time are correct."

He scanned the paper intently, then nodded.

"There's a cycle of unpredictability during the next nine months. You won't know what's happening from day to day." This was much like what I'd seen in Lou Ann's chart. It didn't tell me when she would die, but it described the unexpected medical problems she repeatedly encountered. Because Uranus brought the unexpected, I hoped knowing that would help Tom.

We spent the hour talking about how to emotionally prepare his wife and family, and after Tom left I decided to take a closer look at his chart. I respected his commitment to preparing the people who loved him. I thought of the day my mom died, how surprised and shocked I'd been. I still wished my parents had been honest with us.

In studying Lou Ann's death chart, I'd noticed the nodes of the moon were rising and setting, a position of critical importance on anyone's birth or death chart, but with the death chart I'd come to understand these indicated a soul lesson, a step on the individual's evolutionary path. I looked for times when this would happen to Tom, combined with outer planet transits.

I knew that, no matter what I found, I would never share the results with him. This study was for myself. Besides, predicting the time or date of someone's death, even if I could see it clearly on the chart, would be crossing a moral or ethical line, something I'd discussed with the few colleagues who also experienced people asking them to predict a death.

Over the years I'd urged people to travel to see ailing family members and say goodbye or visit their doctors before they were sick. I'd even told someone she had to get her son into chemical dependency treatment right away. But every one of those choices was in service of my client. Predicting an exact time of death seemed impossible, and I couldn't see how or who it would help. I'd only found two astrology books written about predicting death, and they were simplistic and formulaic. What about people on life support, or in the final throes of Alzheimer's? Were they still actually alive? Would their charts reflect that uncertainty? Would Tom do more to get his life in order if he had an expiration date? From watching Lou Ann, I didn't think so.

All the time I was thinking about Tom's chart and his terrible dilemma, I was also wrapped up in matters at home. Over the last weeks our cat Leo had shied away from eating, stopped grooming, and barely left his bed. Now he was sixteen years old and had lived with us since he was a kitten. For days, I'd worried about him, sharing bits of our salmon and chicken from dinner, letting him sleep on our bed, giving him extra love. So I wasn't completely surprised when I got home and Mindy ushered me into the back room to talk.

"We need to call the vet." She reached for my hand, her voice full of tears. "Leo is refusing food and water."

Leo had been a rescue, a light gray shorthair with the softest fur. He had the loudest purr of any cat I'd known, and often when I stopped petting him, he'd lick my hand for more. I walked over to his plush, maroon cat bed, a gift from Mindy's mom during one of her annual visits. He was curled into a tight little ball. Usually when he heard my voice he'd respond, but now there was nothing. I sat down and petted his matted coat. The very first time I adopted a cat my vet told me that I would be responsible for not only her life but her death. She explained that cats were masters at hiding pain, and owners were ethically bound to relieve their suffering. Now Leo was in our hands, waiting for our loving decision. Mindy said she'd call the vet.

We took turns checking on him that night, giving him water from a dropper, and listening for changes in his breathing. The second time my alarm buzzed I was reminded of the night at Lou Ann's house: I had the same exact feeling in my body, a strange mix of dread and awareness that something important was approaching. Holding the dropper for Leo, I also found myself thinking of Tom, who was edging his way toward this moment in his own way. I wondered how his conversation with his family had gone.

I woke Ana and Della a little early to say their goodbyes to Leo before leaving for school. As tears ran down their cheeks, we each shared a favorite Leo story. It was five-year-old Ana who remembered that young Leo used to play fetch with his cat toys, bringing them back to our feet, hoping we'd throw them again.

My favorite vet, Jen, showed up after the kids left. Our clinic made house calls by request. Leo hadn't moved from his cat bed overnight, and I knew we'd made the right decision. Jen followed us up to our bedroom.

"Do you need a moment?" Jen asked.

I looked at Mindy, who shook her head and said no. We'd said our goodbyes earlier, as a family.

Jen took out a syringe and attached a needle. "Leo won't feel any pain," she said. "It will be just like falling asleep." She looked at us. "Are you ready?"

"Ready," Mindy said, grabbing my hand and squeezing.

I kept hold of Mindy and leaned over to put my other hand on Leo's back, finding a soft spot where his fur was still silken. Mindy cupped his head. Silently I thanked him for all his years of love and friendship. Jen pulled some loose skin on Leo's scruff and slowly injected the contents of the syringe. I watched as Leo's body changed, his fast breathing slowed and stopped, and his body gradually unwound. "He's gone," Jen said.

Seeing my beloved companion so still reminded me of Lou Ann's unmoving corpse. The moment the door closed behind Jen, sobs wracked my body. Who would curl up on my lap during the cold of winter? Who would lick my hand when he wanted more petting? I still wasn't sure how I would live without Lou Ann, and now Leo was gone too. I thought about running a death chart for Leo, but we'd chosen his time of death. That was a new twist on the death chart work I'd been learning and practicing, I realized. Something to think more about later.

Jen returned with a cat carrier and left with Leo's body. Once she left, I turned to embrace Mindy as we sobbed together. I held her tight, until she quieted. "He was a great cat," I said, "and at least we got to say goodbye."

43

Planting a Maple Tree

Elizabeth and I planned a gathering to mark the one-year anniversary of Lou Ann's death. I contacted the care team, newly aware of how much each person loved my twin and how much they had sacrificed during her illness and death. I'd made everyone a card using watercolors, feathers, shells, and small beads, with a specific thank you inside each one.

We were just six, the key people in Lou Ann's final days. In the hot afternoon sun, I arrived late at Elizabeth's house—no longer Lou Ann's house, I told myself. Sweat trickled down my forehead and leaked into my eyes. Children's shouts from the nearby playground carried across the grassy hills.

Elizabeth led us to the park. She'd bought a young maple tree, and with the park's permission we were going to plant it with Lou Ann's ashes. The tree already lay on its side and a shovel was nearby. Karen began to dig the hole, and we passed the shovel around until a round black gash of darkness marked the green grass.

I handed everyone a small slip of paper and a pencil. "Write a wish for your healing, or a message for Lou Ann," I said, "and we'll plant them with the tree." From a boom box, Vivaldi's "Four Seasons" began to play. Everyone bent their heads to the task.

Elizabeth took out a glass jar from the Cremation Society containing gray powder and white bone fragments. I looked at the jar but couldn't connect it with Lou Ann. If she was near, it wasn't because of her ashes in a jar.

"I'll go first," Judith said. She took a trowel with some dirt, sprinkled it with a bit of Lou Ann's ashes, and placed it by the roots of the now upright tree. "I love you and miss you," she whispered, placing her paper into the hole. The music reached a crescendo and then softened. Karen went next, and then Jesse (Karen's long-term partner), Patrick, and Elizabeth, until everyone but me had buried their wishes with some ashes.

I stepped close to the young tree, admiring its dark green leaves and shiny bark. "Grow big and strong and keep her planted in our memories," I told it. I buried my note with Lou Ann's ashes, listening for anything she might send back, feeling a hollowness in my stomach when nothing came. I'd gotten a few moments with her over the past year, thanks to the homeopathic remedy and Gayle's therapy, and my grief was now more like a constant sea spray than the overwhelming force of ocean waves.

Everyone stepped close and, using their feet, pushed the rest of the dirt around the base of the tree until the maple stood tall. After I read from Psalm 23, Elizabeth read Marge Piercy's version of the mourner's kaddish. Then we stood for a moment, each of us silent in our own thoughts until we walked back to Elizabeth's house.

I gathered everyone in front of the computer and slipped in the DVD I'd made. It was a short video from 2001 when Ana was sixteen months old and Mindy, the kids, and I had returned from living in France. Lou Ann, a proud aunt, visited us often, wanting to make up for missed time with both kids. I remember how happy I was to see her instant bond with my children with none of the distance or anger our mother often showed us. Both Lou Ann and I had worked hard to change the family legacy.

The disk whirred and clicked, and there she was, walking through our dining room to Ana, who sat on the couch surrounded by soft cushions. "There you are, sweetie," she said, leaning over to pick up the baby, kissing her neck and cheek.

In the video Lou Ann's thick hair was that luxurious brunette color I knew so well. Same as mine. Her mouth moved with the same expressions as my mouth, her hands looked identical to mine as she held Ana up in the air and Ana giggled with delight.

Cremation is such an odd process. Down the street, in a park I always passed on the way to this house, lay the last bits of my sister's physical body. But here she was on the screen and in our hearts, alive in memory. "Doesn't she look good?" someone said. "Listen to her voice," another said. Then, "her hair, it's so thick."

I touched my own hair, smoothing it back from my forehead, smiling a little to myself. Lou Ann was still here, with people who loved her.

44

Twinless Twins

"Can I sit here?" The young woman wore a high ponytail. Her name tag read, "Alana twin to Elena." She leaned forward and looked at my name tag. "Linda twin to Lou Ann, is this your first conference?"

Twinless Twins had been meeting annually for ten years but, of course, I hadn't needed to come before. I nodded.

"My third." She sat down. When did your twin die?"

"A year ago. Ovarian cancer." I felt a familiar tightness in my throat.

"Three years ago for me. Car accident." She blinked fast, looking past me at the almost one hundred people crowded into this hotel ballroom in Delray Beach. "It helps, coming here."

I had discovered the Twinless Twins conference on the internet about six months earlier and decided to make the journey. I hadn't tried any other support groups after the one at the church, but something in me wanted to be among others who had experienced twin loss.

Alana twin to Elena joined the others as the meeting started. We took turns walking to the microphone and talking about our twins, how they died, our grief, and the painstaking recovery.

Everyone's experience echoed what I'd been through with Lou Ann: shock, disbelief, and profound grief. The featureless meeting room with its cushioned chairs and chandeliers blazing overhead became a pain-filled container in the days that followed. Listening to other twins' stories was so agonizing that my grief felt heavier.

Some stories were violent, others full of extended suffering. One woman went to visit her twin, who lived just a mile away, to find she'd been murdered by the husband she'd recently divorced. Another man had to make the decision to take his brother off life support after a motorcycle accident.

Over the next two days I spent more time alone in my room, feeling sunk. I was with people who shared my loss, yet I was unable to get close to anyone. And Lou Ann, even though I'd talked about her with a few people, seemed further away.

The keynote speaker was a licensed psychologist from New York City whose twin brother had died thirty-five years earlier. As she gathered her notes at the podium, something in her posture reminded me of Mom, and when she looked up the likeness was striking: her brown eyes reflected a deep sadness, a look I saw on Mom's face when she thought I wasn't watching. "Everyone grieves differently," she told us, "so don't judge yourself. All of your feelings are normal." I knew she was right about that. She paused and scanned the room, caught my eyes and held them for a second. "Remember, you will heal from this loss," she added, as if she were addressing me alone, "even though it's hard, and it takes time."

As I returned to my room, I wondered about the sense of familiarity. The speaker was the same height and body type as Mom, but it was her aura of loneliness that caught my attention, as if she carried a great tragedy. I remembered how, as a young teen, I'd overheard my parents fighting. Anguish filled Mom's voice as I heard her screaming about how Dad would never understand her. At that moment I didn't know what she meant, but in adulthood I did.

The closing ceremony was a candle-lighting ritual at dusk in the courtyard. The air in the brick courtyard was warm and unnaturally still, as if nature were holding her breath. As we filed into the outdoor space, volunteers handed us each a small candle wrapped in a paper plate. Everyone spread out, facing each other in a large circle.

A Josh Groban ballad about lost love played on the overhead speakers while someone suggested we use this time to remember our twin. Then a woman walked around lighting each small candle from her big one. I shifted from foot to foot, waiting my turn, wiping the sweat running down my face with a tissue.

Gradually the sky grew dark. The courtyard filled with many small flickering lights, then cries and sobs as the music swelled. Candlelight illuminated the faces of each twin, casting shadows on the walls behind them. In the shadows, each missing twin came into view. Seeing so many lost twins, I broke into sobs. Why could I see other people's twins but not Lou Ann?

Then the woman next to me grabbed my hand, squeezing gently, and something changed. I felt it in my body as a beneficence. My breathing slowed; the sobs calmed. *We're all in this together*, I thought.

That's when I heard Lou Ann's heartbeat, echoing mine.

My entire life, I'd imagined growing old with my sister, sharing our childhood memories, and continuing to fill the places left empty by Mom's death. All of us standing in this circle had imagined the same thing, I realized. Every twin here had thought, "Because we were born together, we'd die together."

I squeezed the hand in mine and let it fall, gripping my candle a little tighter.

**

Two years later the conference was meeting in Minneapolis, and I'd volunteered to be on the planning committee, using my association with Gayle to bring grief therapists into breakout groups.

"We even took turns driving to work together," Joan twin to Jane said, wiping the tears from her chin. "No one understands. I lost my sister, my best friend, along with my work and carpool buddy."

I looked around the circle of about twenty people, and everyone was nodding their agreement. I tried to imagine how I would recover if Lou Ann and I had lived and worked together, but couldn't. In spite of that, this conference was already different. Gayle was here along with two colleagues, and they had the capacity to help people start to heal.

"Are any of your coworkers supportive?" Gayle asked.

"They don't miss Jane anymore, so they think I should be over it."

"That happens to me too," John twin to Dawn said, "but it's my family."

"Grief never completely goes away." Gayle said. "When you feel the pain and accept the loss, it can become less consuming." She looked at everyone sitting in the circle. "Those of us who study death and grief realize that having a deadline for recovery never works. It's more important to take care of yourself with regular meals, sleep, and exercise, and get support from someone you trust."

After spending time at Twinless Twins conferences, I began to understand how similar Lou Ann and I were to most other twins. Many twins spoke of having telepathy, knowing their twin was hurt or had just died, or being visited by their twin at the time of death. They also shared experiences of buying the same outfits for special occasions or the same gifts for friends, or having identical conversations with family members. Many struggled with family favoritism, jealousy, and competition with their sibling, and problems with their twin's spouse. All of these themes had been part of our lives.

45

Lou Ann Visits

Something profound changed in me after spending time at Twinless Twins. I awoke a few weeks later from the dream I'd longed for since my sister's death.

"Lou Ann came to me last night," I told Mindy over coffee that morning. We sat on our soft blue couch in the living room. I could hear Della and Ana playing upstairs, punctuated by Ana's musical laughter that I loved so much. "My sister's hair was shiny like it used to be, she had flesh on her bones, and her face was soft and relaxed." I took a deep breath, settling back, and Mindy scooted closer to me.

"Tell me more," she said.

"Well, in the dream I'd gone to see a new therapist," I said. "Someone I didn't know. And Lou Ann walked in."

"Really?" Mindy said. "Lou Ann was your new therapist?"

In real life my sister would never have been my therapist. That would be totally unprofessional, but in the dream that didn't matter. "She said she was sorry I had to wait so long, but time was different for her." I took a sip of my coffee, a new dark roast we were trying. I liked it. "I started to cry, and I told her how much I missed her. Then she held me." I leaned into Mindy on the couch. "Her hair smelled like the shampoo she always used."

Mindy placed her hands on mine. They felt warm and solid. "It sounds profound," she said.

"And she gave me a healing, a laying on of hands."

"How do you feel from it?"

I took a moment to check in with myself. "Different. Peaceful. Whole."

I wrote the dream in my journal, covering pages with intricate detail. In the dream, Lou Ann had been accompanied by six beings of light—glowing outlines who chanted and moved their hands over me until I fell into a trance. It was surreal, even for my dreams. And it stayed with me for days and months. Reading and remembering the dream touched off a subtle thrum of connection. A reminder that Lou Ann was close.

I wanted to talk with others who had been through this type of loss, and I'd liked Alana from the Twinless Twins conference, but we didn't connect enough to stay in touch. A few weeks later, Lou Ann's friend Sherri asked me to coffee. Sherri and Lou Ann had gone through the same arduous training to become psychoanalysts, and Sherri had been a constant, reassuring presence during my sister's chemotherapy.

For an hour, we happily reminisced about Lou Ann, both of us obviously missing her, glad to talk about her and remember the quirky, unique person Lou Ann was. Then the tone of the conversation changed. "Lou Ann was mean sometimes," Sherri said as she studied the floor. "The way she always commented on my messiness."

I leaned forward. After her death Lou Ann achieved an almost saint-like status, so this was a surprise. Sherri's glasses fogged up as she sipped her tea, not meeting my eyes. "I could feel her disapproval when I didn't live up to her standards." She shrugged. "I know I'm not the neatest person in the world. But sometimes her disapproval radiated off her in waves."

"Just like our mother," I said. "One look could turn you into a pillar of salt."

Sherri looked up. "Lou Ann talked to me about your critical mother. As psychotherapists, we think we're so self-aware, but that's not always true." She took a breath. "Was your mom self-righteous too? Sometimes Lou Ann got rigid about being right."

"When Lou Ann went into stubborn mode, I learned there was no changing her mind." I sipped my coffee. "At least not right away."

Sherri's phone buzzed, interrupting my next comment. She gave me a look of apology. "Sorry, I have to answer this." She grabbed her phone and hurried away from the table. I remembered Lou Ann getting those phone calls from clients having mental health emergencies, sometimes even needing to be hospitalized. After a few minutes Sherri came back. "I have to run." She grabbed her jacket. "Maybe we can talk again?"

I drove home, thinking about what I'd learned. Obviously, I didn't know everything about my twin. Even with her being older by only twenty-three minutes, I'd put her on a pedestal like so many younger sisters do.

Lou Ann's best friend in high school, Debbie, now lived on the east coast. They'd had a falling-out after college, but I still didn't know why. Shortly after my visit with Sherri, I heard that Debbie would be at our high school reunion in a few weeks. I decided to go.

It wasn't hard to recognize her—a familiar face surrounded by gray hair. We grabbed each other, and her body shook with sobs. I held her tight until they stopped.

"I can't believe she's gone." She straightened up, ending the embrace. "Somehow seeing you without her makes it real."

I knew what I wanted to ask her, but I let a few minutes pass as we chatted about families, children, and work. Then I put my hand on Debbie's arm. "Lou Ann ended your relationship. Did you ever reconcile?"

"Let's sit over there." She pointed toward a bench under a tree, away from the commotion of the reunion. "I'll tell you the whole story," she paused, "even though I still don't understand what happened."

We settled, and I waited. Finally Debbie sighed. "My husband and I have tons of lesbian friends, and our synagogue in Massachusetts is almost half gay. So when Lou Ann left Joe and told me she was in love with a woman, I was totally fine. I invited the two of them over for dinner. That was when we still lived in town." Tears welled in her eyes. "I loved Lou Ann, and I thought we'd be friends forever. But after she came out, she never came over or returned any of my calls." She took a tissue from her purse and wiped her eyes. "I emailed and called, but I never got a response. Any idea why?"

I thought back on that time, the challenges we'd both faced as newly out lesbians, the rejection from our family. How exciting it had been to finally be in love, finally feel like a whole person. But the fragility of our new lives—had Lou Ann felt too exposed, too vulnerable with her past? I knew she'd kept some friends from high school. So why not Debbie?

I shook my head. "I hoped you might have answers."

But it wasn't until I went home that night and pulled out my ephemeris to look up Debbie's birth chart that I found an explanation for myself. Debbie's sun, the planet of illumination, was right on Lou Ann's Uranus, a planet I associated with coming out. The combination spoke of intensity of feelings, a magnetic connection, and an almost unbearable conflict, with Lou Ann wanting more intimacy than Debbie. Even worse, Debbie had fallen in love and gotten married soon after high school.

A memory came. When we were sixteen, Lou Ann had claimed Debbie as her exclusive friend, much to my surprise. She'd said she was too old to share everything and everyone with me, and Debbie was hers. *Ah*, I thought, setting the book aside and turning off my light. *Debbie was Lou Ann's first love*. Once she came out, seeing Debbie married would have been unbearable. Unable to face her feelings, she cut Debbie off.

I remembered Gayle telling me that people die but relationships live on. I wondered if I'd ever be able to tell Debbie the truth about what I'd learned, or if I would need to keep these new insights about my sister to myself.

46

Lost on the Mountain

For my second birthday without Lou Ann, we rented a condo just outside Estes Park, Colorado. Past birthdays held memories of being with my sister. The previous year's birthday, although wonderful, had been diluted by a fog of grief. Even thinking about having a party, or too much fun, felt wrong. How could I celebrate being born without the one I was born with?

I'd hungered for more dreams with Lou Ann, more reassurance that she was still in my inner life, if not my outer. But it had been almost a full year since my dream with her and the light beings.

The first morning in Estes Park, I padded downstairs while the kids still slept and made coffee, bringing a steaming mug to Mindy's bedside table. I kissed her warm cheek and sat down next to her. "I had another dream with her."

"Lou Ann?" Mindy slowly opened her eyes.

"We were preparing for her memorial service together."

"You did that knowing she was dead?" She sat up against the soft headboard and took the coffee I offered.

"It was strange," I said. "In the dream, we sorted through old childhood photos, and she told me that dying was the best time of her life. All her relationships became the most intimate and free from pretense that they had ever been." I stretched out next to Mindy. "Her exact words."

It confused me and it filled me with sadness to think that dying had been the highlight of my sister's life. But it rang true. For years, she'd taken care of others: her patients, Elizabeth, me, my children, her friends, and her coworkers. When she got sick, the world shifted. Everyone focused on her, offering support and love. Eventually she let it in.

Mindy set down her mug and wrapped her arms around me, her steady breathing relaxing my body. I realized I'd fallen asleep again when a clatter from the kitchen woke me up. I was alone in bed. Suddenly, the bedroom door opened. I smelled pancakes.

"Happy birthday to you," sang Mindy, Della, and Ana.

The narrow, winding road to Rocky Mountain National Park took us two thousand feet above the town. We'd brought jackets and hats for the elevation, pulling them on before we started up the hiking path. I was glad to be in the mountains with my family, always grateful that Mindy and I shared this love of the outdoors and of nature, remembering that first canoe trip when I knew we'd spend our lives together. We hiked quietly, the kids running ahead up the path, backpacks bouncing, eventually disappearing into the misty cloud that surrounded us.

"Oh no! We're lost on the mountain," we heard them yelling, and immediately they skipped back into view, only to disappear into the mist again. Both Della and Ana were giggling hard, and their laughter triggered a tiny bubble of lightness inside my chest. Soon we emerged above the clouds to picnic on warm rocks overlooking a distant blue lake.

Lou Ann would have loved this, I thought. I remembered the fast pace she had set when we hiked in this same park years earlier, keeping me panting and breathless. Her strength and fitness back then put me to shame. She'd seemed so healthy.

On the drive down the mountain into Estes Park for dinner, we saw a large group of elk grazing close to the road. I eased the rental car onto the shoulder for a better look. A buck with a big rack lumbered toward us, stopping about twenty feet from the car. He faced us and stomped the ground with his two front hooves, nostrils flaring. The challenge was clear, so I put the car into drive, and we coasted away.

After dinner we changed into swimsuits, and I found a flashlight by the back door. One by one in the solitary beam, we shivered our way down narrow wooden stairs to the hot tub. On both sides, underwater lights shimmered a luminescent aqua color and steam rose from the water. Mindy, Della, and I stepped into the tub and eased our bodies all the way into the hot water, sighing and crooning. Ana found a perch on one side and dangled her feet in the water.

Leaning back, I looked up at the sky. A giant paintbrush of glitter made one grand stroke across a deep midnight blue canvas. "Can you see the Milky Way?" I asked softly. Della leaned toward Ana and pointed directly above. "Up there."

"So pretty," they said in unison. We sat in silence for a moment.

The deep quiet and soothing warmth made it hard to stay awake, and soon I was nestled up against Mindy on the couch, both kids sleeping peacefully in the next room.

"Thanks for a wonderful birthday," I said. "I had a good day."

"Not too sad about Lou Ann?"

"Yes and no. I keep seeing that eclipse in our charts, remembering the day I knew she would die." I rubbed my eyes. "How fast and chaotic it would be because of what I saw there."

She pulled the fleece blanket from the top of the couch and covered our legs.

"What?" Mindy didn't have a passion for astrology anymore, but her voice, so soft and gentle, encouraged me to talk more about mine.

"Well," I began, "I knew I was in for a separation with Uranus opposite my sun." I shook my head. "Uranus was the marker for that terrible car crash back in 1995, remember?"

"I remember you saying that," Mindy looked at her hands. "Those were dark days for sure. Our first baby, my dad dying, and you on crutches for months." The white hot pain in my foot, radiating up my leg, kept me from holding baby Della longer than a few minutes.

I put my head on Mindy's shoulder. "We were both so burdened and desperate in different ways."

"But we made it through," she said. "Just like we will now. Because you're one of the bravest people I know."

47
Student Art Show

I'd never thought of myself as an artist. That title belonged to Lou Ann. Her success as a potter was legend in our community and her raku pots were prized by friends and customers. I never questioned it, never imagined I would begin my own journey with art. Not until I sat as a model during a friend's portrait class. It was then I realized I wanted to study painting.

I had taken classes regularly for nine years, sharing my work with my sister, fighting against a sense of competition, since I knew she thought my still lifes were pretty, but nothing on the scale of what she created. In 2002, while she was still alive, I created a series of four paintings named *Going, Going, Gone*. Using apple halves as symbols for Lou Ann and myself, I painted them further and further apart until they were just hints of color on the edge of the canvas. When my teacher asked me to interpret the series, I told her it showed how having children changed my relationship with my twin. My teacher often said that the subconscious emerged through art, and even then I knew the series was about much more—something I could not yet articulate.

After Lou Ann's death in 2005, I completed a group of pastels called *The Grief Series*. Like *Going, Going, Gone*, many of them had two apple halves, but rather than being separated by a nature scene, they were kept apart by a barrier. Some barriers were permeable, others solid. I wasn't showing them to make a sale; the act of creating the paintings had been enough, emotional and deeply cathartic. Still, I had chosen to take part in the student show.

The day of the show arrived. Art students, family, and friends crowded into the classroom studio and spilled into the hall. In a corner next to my paintings I nestled an altar to Lou Ann, displaying two of her small raku pots. I'd just finished lighting a memorial candle when a young, red-haired woman approached me.

"Lou Ann!" A bright smile lit her face. "It's been ages. How are you?"

This was a frequent occurrence when Lou Ann was alive, but a first since she died.

I felt the familiar pressure behind my eyes. "I'm sorry, you've mistaken me for my sister. I'm Lou Ann's twin."

"Sorry," her smile began to fade. "I didn't know she had a twin." The woman leaned toward the wall and read my artist statement. "Lou Ann died? Oh no." Tears leaked down her cheeks. "Excuse me." As the woman hurried away, Mindy came up and put her arms around me. We stood together until my composure returned.

THE BIG BROWN cardboard box was on the dining room table when I came home from my student show. Both kids were in bed, and Mindy's phone voice filtered in from the back room. I sat down at the table, opened the box, and pulled out a picture of Lou Ann and me in front the Whitney Museum in Manhattan. We were around forty. Lou Ann wore a permanent; my hair was straight. Even so, our features, posture, the tilt of our heads, were identical. I remembered how we covered the long city blocks with our fast walk, the Jewish delis where we ate corned beef on rye with spicy mustard, the windy ferry ride we took around the Statue of Liberty. We had talked, laughed, and explored side-by-side, a team of two ready for anything.

It was on the way home I had another one of my "knowings." We'd parted at Grand Central Station, where I was taking a train to visit a friend. The ticket line was long, and voices echoed off the high ceilings. As I inched my way toward the counter, a tall, well-dressed man suddenly stepped in front of me.

"Ma'am, you need to help me." His nervous hands touched his jacket, his hair, and his pockets. "I lost my wallet. My bus is leaving. Ten dollars?" He never met my eyes and with every word his movements became more erratic. I hesitated. He stepped closer and lowered his voice. "I asked you real nice." I opened my purse and pulled out some money.

"Here, that's all I have."

Relief washed through me as he hurried off into the crowd. Not an un-usual thing in this city, I supposed, about to shrug it off. Then a shiver ran up my back. I thought of Lou Ann, and I knew something was wrong. As soon as I could after I arrived at my friend's home, I called. Her voice was strained.

"I was mugged on the way to the plane," she said. "One guy tackled me, and the other one ran off with my purse. Everyone just watched, and no one helped."

"Shit!" I paced up and down across my friend's living room, as far as the phone cord could stretch. "What did you do?"

"Put myself at the mercy of the gate agent until he found the record of my purchase. He let me board without a ticket. I still don't have my ID or anything else." She blew out a long breath. "But at least I'm alive."

A few months after the show, I decided to photograph all my apple paint-ings. I started with the first one I'd painted, two apples halves side by side. Looking at it that day, I realized the painting captured how I understood myself in relationship to Lou Ann. Her half was bigger, facing front, and it expressed confidence and self-assurance. In contrast, my apple half took up less space; it was turned to the side, not quite as bright. I loved my sis-ter with all my heart, but back then I often wondered why everything in her life seemed easier, shinier, forward-facing. It wasn't until 2014, when I learned that Ana had attachment issues stemming from her adoption and I studied them in depth, that I understood the consequences of my being left in the incubator. Those earliest days of skin-to-skin contact with the family allow an infant to develop a secure sense of self and ability to bond.

"What're you doing?" Della leaned over my shoulder, looking at the photos.

"Making a book to help remember my twin."

I opened my laptop, scrolling through a selection of black and whites. "Which ones do you like?"

Della leaned forward. "The one of you two in high chairs with those matching bibs and that one, where I can't even tell you apart."

Della stayed with me for an hour, helping me choose. I uploaded our childhood photos, imagining what I'd say about each to honor everything Lou Ann meant to me. To acknowledge how far I'd come since her death. The book would be a marker of my personal, private progress, but also a gift to share with those who also loved my sister. A way to remember how close we were and how far apart we were now. And also a reminder that I could be a whole person myself. By the end of two days, I had created a small, thirty-page book, *A Tale of Two Sisters*. Publishing it, putting out a personal statement for the world to see, made Lou Ann's death more real. But I sensed even bigger changes were about to happen.

48

Dad's Secret

*I*n another dream a few years after Lou Ann's death, I went to a large hotel for a conference on the intersection of traditional and alternative therapies, a subject that interested both my twin and me. After a short introduction in a large ballroom, I followed a map to find my small breakout group. I was first to enter the room and took a seat in an empty circle of chairs. Then Lou Ann walked in. We were equally delighted and surprised to see each other.

Soon the room filled with middle-aged professionals. We were introduced to new healing techniques, and the teacher assigned us to small groups to practice. Every twenty minutes we changed groups. Lou Ann and I were in some groups together, and those were by far the most interesting. The hour-long session ended. When I walked to the door to get out of the room, I had to peel back layers of gauze. Relieved to be on the other side of the weird doorway, I turned to help Lou Ann through. She was gone. The gauze had closed. As much as I wanted her close, we couldn't be together as we had been before.

Weeks later, I had an urge to search in my files for the grief paintings I'd made. In them, I'd painted symbols to represent the separation between myself and my twin. One of the barriers looked exactly like the gauze doorway in my dream.

When my family and I went to visit Aunt Dianne later that week, I thought about telling her the dream. I wondered if she had ever experienced a separation with her twin. I knew they'd lived in different cities for a while. But I didn't tell her. My dream felt private, personal, just for me.

Aunt Dianne leaned across the table, lowering her voice. We'd managed to include this quick visit to Denver as part of our summer vacation. I was grateful Ana and Della were playing in her backyard while Mindy and I drank coffee with her in her bright, sunny kitchen. I knew she had something important to tell me, something I needed to know now that my father was dying.

Dianne took a deep breath. "Your dad's father murdered his second wife by bludgeoning her to death with a hammer."

I sat back in shock. I had known that my grandmother, his first wife, divorced him because he was abusive, but this went way beyond that.

Dianne nodded. "He held a knife to your grandmother's throat during sex. That's why she divorced him—that and the beatings." She walked to the stove and poured herself more coffee. I could see her hands trembling. How long had she'd known this, kept it to herself? "My Rueben had a temper, but he was a kind man. Your father is too."

Mindy was frowning at her phone. "Do you remember the year of the murder, and where he was living?"

"Los Angeles. 1948."

On her phone, Mindy showed me a newspaper article from the *Los Angeles Times:* "Man seeks death after hammer killing of wife." I peered at the grainy black and white photo of a man with his head wrapped with a white bandage. Dad resembled him around the mouth and chin.

**

"Dad," I called as I let myself into his tiny apartment in the assisted living complex. I could see him asleep in his wheelchair. Bits of dried food stained his sweater and his wispy gray hair lay matted against the side of his head. Since Henrietta had died a couple months earlier, he'd gone downhill fast, telling me he had no reason to live. When I reminded him he still had me, Mark, and two lovely grandchildren, he couldn't meet my eyes.

"Dad, wake up." I opened the curtains, then the window. The room smelled stale. "It's a beautiful day and I'm taking you outside."

He opened his eyes. "Linda. It's you."

I grabbed his jacket from the closet. "Let me help you put this on. I think you'll enjoy being out in the sun."

An electric door opener let us into the courtyard. I wheeled him into a sitting area surrounded by a manicured garden. Today the magnolia tree was in bloom and some purple crocuses brightened the fresh mulch.

"Push me into the sun?" he asked. I turned his wheelchair so the sun would be at his back and pulled up a white plastic chair to sit next to him. I'd begun to savor my visits with him, now that it was clear that our time together was limited.

"I talked with your grandmother the other day," he said. "She's doing well."

His mother had been dead for nearly thirty years.

"You been talking to anyone else?"

"Pearl drops by now and again. We share a cherry coke."

"That's nice." I took a deep breath. Aunt Pearl had loved her cherry cokes. "What about Lou Ann?"

No answer. His head drooped onto his chest, and I could hear his slow, steady breathing. He'd fallen asleep.

We sat in silence for a while. I watched a robin struggle to pull a fat worm out of the grass, let the time pass, and thought about what Dianne had shared. I realized again that my mother's violence paralleled my father's life as a child. Perhaps that was one reason he'd not intervened.

Dad's head came back up. "Must've drifted off." He peered up at me. "I'm cold. Take me back inside so I can sleep?"

After I got him in bed, I leaned over and kissed his cheek. His eyes flickered open. "Linda," he murmured, "you're a good girl."

WHEN MY DAD died, I wasn't there. I'd spent a few hours at his bedside, listening to the fluid in his lungs rattle as they filled up. He'd entered a coma and seemed at peace. At ninety-four years old, he had told me many times that he was ready. It was my brother Mark who slept on the floor in the nursing unit and called me the next morning to say that Dad was gone. I jotted down the time and created a death chart for him a month later, but there was nothing beyond what I already knew: he was depressed and tired of living. Looking at his death chart, I waited to feel the expected rush of grief, or the reopening of the barely stitched together wound of losing Lou Ann, but it never came.

At our father's funeral, I missed Lou Ann terribly. On the day Mark and I cleaned out his apartment, her absence hurt my heart. But between my father and myself, something had healed. In the act of parenting my parent, I saw the fragile child inside my father and forgave him.

49

Our Wedding

Mindy and I sat on our back deck, surrounded by the smell of lilies and the sound of a mower humming quietly in the distance as I studied my new astrology app, searching for the best possible date for our wedding. After twenty-two years, we were able to marry legally. It felt like a miracle, and it felt long overdue. Snippets of canned laughter from the TV show the kids were watching floated through the screen door.

"Min!" I had to say her name twice, her head was buried so deep inside the newspaper. "I found the perfect date in November." Symbols spread out around the typical chart wheel in a large kite pattern. I tilted the screen toward her.

From my years reading charts, I knew all the many patterns that could appear: T-squares, grand squares, grand trines, and yods each meant something different to the experienced astrologer. But a kite pattern was very desirable. It symbolized good energy balanced by a tiny bit of stress. A chart without any stress creates too much stasis—never a good thing for a marriage. And a little bit of stress accurately reflected who we were as a couple.

Being a same-sex couple came with its own particular kind of stress. Until recently, laws had mostly made us invisible. We celebrated our love privately and enjoyed the victories when they came. I remembered the joyous day four months earlier when we stood with Ana and Della at the state capitol in 2013, watching Governor Dayton sign the freedom-to-marry law, surrounded by hundreds of same-sex couples. Mindy and I had hugged so hard I thought I would explode. That August when the law took effect statewide, we started wedding plans.

My wife-to-be bent over the iPad. "Remind me what's good about it."

I loved it when she asked specific astrology questions. I grinned at her. "Almost all the planets are in fire, which is playful and outgoing, and in air, which is social and communicative. If we set the wedding for November 17, the moon is in Libra and Venus will make supportive contacts to both of our charts."

She grinned back at me. "Moon and Venus are good, right?"

"Moon in Libra is the best possible sign for a wedding." I squeezed her hand.

She leaned back in her deck chair and sighed. "I never thought this would happen in our lifetime."

"Me either." A quiet moment passed. "We'll create a new anniversary, one without reminders of loss." Lou Ann had died two days after we usually celebrated our anniversary. For the past eight years, we'd given each other cards but that was all. I leaned forward, newly filled with appreciation for Mindy, who had patiently and lovingly weathered my grieving. "With a wedding in November, I won't be thinking of Lou Ann, only you."

We kissed.

**

Smiling friends swiveled in their seats, a sea of welcome and goodwill. The Hebrew words and the familiar melody of "Erev Shel Shoshanim," our wedding processional, stirred up memories of singing with Lou Ann at summer camp, the soft waves lapping on the lake, and the glittering nighttime stars. But now it was Mindy's hand that was warm in mine as we walked down the sanctuary aisle. Our community had gathered to celebrate us, these dear friends from every part of my life replacing the family I no longer had. Lou Ann had died eight years earlier, it had been four years since Dad had died, and forty-seven years had passed since Mom's death.

I glanced at the remembrance table we'd created on the altar. A small decorative raku teapot that Lou Ann had made glowed like a flame, surrounded by Dad's watch, Mom's china teacup, and a photo of Mindy's father. I felt their presence in the room like the sound of a distant river, always moving through my life.

In front of the bimah, the room's central platform, we stopped and faced each other. We'd practiced this. But in the moment, the reality made my heart ache with joy. Mindy's brown eyes glowed with light as I slowly circled her three times, imagining wrapping a warm soft shawl of my love around her. Each time I came back to those smiling eyes. She walked around me three times, too, binding our union with her protection and love. We completed the circle with each other for the seventh and final time.

When we joined hands again I felt different. Safe and whole.

We climbed the two small steps to join Della, Ana, Mindy's two sisters, and the rabbi under the chuppah, the overhead canopy. The small space felt like a nest, and in the air around us lingered sweet notes of just-finished songs. We signed certificates, drank wine, received blessings from our congregations and friends, and exchanged vows and rings, all the while holding and returning to each other's eyes.

"By the power vested in me by God and the state of Minnesota, I now pronounce you married." The rabbi's smile stretched even further as Mindy put her hands on both of my cheeks, and we kissed. Her lips were warm and soft. There was a smattering of applause.

"Go ahead and let them know how you feel," the rabbi said. The room filled with applause and then whistling and cheers. "Twenty-two years they've waited for this." Cheering and clapping got even louder. I laughed into Mindy's neck, already wet from my tears. She squeezed me tighter, and we rocked each other back and forth. I opened my eyes and over her shoulder saw our children. Della's face glowed like a rising sun.

Two napkin-wrapped wine glasses were placed on the floor by our feet. "As a symbol of the fragility of life," the rabbi said, "the brides will each crush a glass." I knew all about the fragility of life, as I felt the thin thrum of connection with my twin. Mindy stomped down, and her glass made a satisfying pop. I lifted my right foot, took aim, and felt the glass shatter underneath my heel.

50

The First Step

Two years after our wedding, the idea of doing death charts for clients began to fascinate me. I had never heard of any astrologer doing them. I could see the challenges, both ethically and practically. I would never create them for the living, only for those who had passed. They were helpful, certainly, for survivors aching to put reason to the sudden or confusing death of a loved one. My forty years of experience would allow me to read the nuances accurately, I felt, but I could only know if I practiced first.

After a few months of ruminating about going public, I thought about clients I could ask. I composed a careful email, explaining what I was offering and asking for volunteers from a select number who trusted my work and would honor the sacredness of the project. Of course, I also had to study my Solar Return chart, a chart specific for my birthday and upcoming birth year, to find a good time to launch my test. The time was promising: an easier year lay ahead emotionally, with the hint of a new idea taking hold in my professional life. With that confirmation I clicked the send button on my group email and waited. Within minutes, fifteen people had volunteered to let me practice reading death charts for them.

From the first reading, though, I knew I was in for a wild ride. Alice had worked with me for ten years. When she came in for her death chart appointment, I knew she wanted to talk about her mother, who had died of cancer four years earlier. It still haunted Alice. As soon as I handed her the chart, she began to talk. She talked for the first half hour without pause. I heard the story of her mom's diagnosis, the trips to the doctor, the second opinion. Such an outpouring of words, almost a venting, hadn't happened since the very early days in my profession. Over the years, I'd learned that when people were frightened about what I might say, they would fill up the time with nonstop talking. It wasn't until they were putting on their coats or walking out the door that I would hear their real stories: "Oh, by the way, we're getting a divorce" or "My wife was diagnosed with lymphoma last week."

I decided to intervene. "Alice, I'd like to say something." She looked at me and stopped talking. "I have information about what your mom experienced right before she died. Would you like to hear that?"

She glanced down, twisting her hands in her lap. "I have to tell you one more thing." She launched into another long story about a dispute between her mom and her sister. The next time she stopped to take a breath I spoke again. "Alice, I'm sorry to tell you, but our time is up."

She stopped talking. The room seemed loud with her silence. "No one has ever listened to the entire story before," she said softly. "I really needed to tell someone."

After she left, I wandered around my office. What had just happened? I didn't think she had talked nonstop to avoid what I had to say. I'd learned some very interesting information doing the chart for her mom, but I realized what I had to say didn't matter. I remembered my sense of relief during my first therapy session with Gayle, how she listened. I opened a new document on my computer and labeled it "Things to remember during death chart readings." I typed one word: listen.

**

Brie's brother had died a few months earlier. She'd already shared with me that she struggled with addiction. She was living sober, but her brother had been in and out of treatment. When she came into my office, I saw the same apprehension on her face as I'd noticed in Alice. *Listen*, I reminded myself.

I wasn't really in the mood to listen, though. I'd woken that morning from a dream in which I'd been hugging Lou Ann, hearing her bright laughter, and I felt empty and aching inside. Still lying in bed, I tried to work backward, to remember more of the dream, but it was already gone. What had we been laughing about? No one could make me laugh like Lou Ann. She'd say something silly, clever, or sarcastic, and I'd start giggling; then she'd look at me and point, and I'd laugh harder. Soon we'd both be holding our stomachs. Feelings of missing her rolled over me like ocean waves.

As I explained how I saw addiction at work in Brie's brother's death chart, I noticed she was looking out the window. I stopped in the middle of explaining Neptune across from his sun and put the chart down. Time to listen, I thought.

"Brie, you seem distracted," I said. "What's going on?"

"Oh, sorry." She ran her hands down the front of her sweater, brushing away something I couldn't see. "It's been an awful time since my brother's death." Her voice got faint as if she was revealing a terrible secret. "I can't stop eating. I even wake up in the middle of the night to eat." She took a Kleenex out of her purse.

"I'm working the steps and going to an extra AA meeting a week, but I'm afraid I'm switching addictions." She wiped her eyes.

Outside, the traffic hummed. I looked at a branch of the maple tree by the window and thought of my sister and how empty I'd felt when she first died. Even now, the emptiness led me into small moments of unconsciousness, like my own mindless eating that morning. "As you heal, the overeating will stop," I told Brie. "It's just been a few months."

"I hope you're right." She leaned over and picked up the chart I'd given her. "I'm ready to hear about Neptune."

We talked about how the death chart revealed her brother's desire to escape his life. I told Brie it was active on the day of his death, and I pointed out terrible anger and impulsiveness with Mars's position in his chart. She studied the arrangement of planets, so descriptive to me, so foreign to most of my clients. *I read these charts like archaeologists read hieroglyphics*, I thought.

"I found a letter from his insurance company denying coverage for a treatment program he'd finished," she said slowly. "He'd checked into treatment knowing he couldn't afford it. Not getting the money sure made him mad." Her eyes filled with tears again. "The police told me he'd been drinking at a neighborhood bar and hit a tree while driving home." She sat for a moment, then wiped her eyes. "He was a block from his house. One block. I'd like to believe the whole thing was impulsive."

On the way home, I thought a lot about Brie's brother as I passed familiar landmarks and thought about going home to my family. He had nobody waiting for him, which must have been a huge disappointment fueling his recklessness, but I wondered if the outcome would have been different if his insurance company had paid for treatment. Karma, a person's destiny based on cause and effect in this life and other lives, was not as clear in his chart compared to others I'd seen. Were the positions of Mars and Neptune enough to warrant what happened to him? I'd never know. But I did know that I still had much to learn in my new study.

I thought about the dream with Lou Ann I'd had that morning. How lost and sad I'd felt afterward. How the sound of her laugh had haunted me most of the day, a longing underneath each death chart I'd examined.

51

Mom's Chart

Another disturbing dream woke me again a week later. In it, my mother was frantically looking for a missing, teenage Lou Ann. No matter what I did to help, she got mad.

At work that day, each of my three clients talked about mothers or dreams. When I unexpectedly got a free hour before I had to be home, I decided to study Mom's death chart. Pulling my office chair over to the computer, I double-clicked on the icon of a sun at the bottom of my screen and went to the drop-down menu to select "new chart." I couldn't remember which year she'd died, so I took out a pen and paper and did the math. I'd never forget that it was New Year's Day, usually a time for new beginnings, and I knew I was seventeen. That made it January 1, 1966. I entered the time, noon, which was an approximation from the time Dad came home with the bad news, and then finally Minneapolis, the city where she died. Those were the basic elements required to generate a chart, for both birth and death.

All it took was one click, and the round wheels full of symbols appeared on the screen. I love these wheels and know them as well as I know the lines on my palm. I've worked with thousands of them, in different configurations, over the forty years of my work life. But each time I create a new chart, I'm filled with curiosity and wonder, never knowing what will appear for each client, how the planets and zodiac will align.

On my mom's death chart, I certainly didn't expect what I saw that morning. In the innermost circle, four red lines made up a grand cross, an indication of incredible tension. It looked like a big red square in the center of everything. I'd seen this only a few times before, in the birth charts of people living with extreme distress. Even one square in a chart indicated conflict, and this chart had four, along with two oppositions, indicators of polarizing extremes. Poor Mom, I thought. Her death mirrored her life, and both were fraught with difficulties. The four conflicts were Saturn conjunct to Chiron, and opposite both Uranus and Pluto, square with Mars. Saturn usually indicated life's hardest lessons, so when it was next to or opposite another heavy hitter, like these three, it meant all the big players in the heavens were at odds with each other, pushing and pulling to gain control.

I took the chart to my desk and pulled out my ephemeris. The sunlight caught the cover and brought back memories of sitting with Diane near Coffman Union and how she talked about Mom and a dark shadow. Outside the window, golden-yellow maple leaves swayed in the breeze, but my mind was racing. I knew eclipses of the sun or moon were often part of this intensity in a death chart, and they would give me a deeper understanding about Mom's inner turmoil.

It took some time to find them, but the eclipses of 1965 lined up with Saturn and the moon/Pluto conjunction in my chart. I closed the book slowly, sat for a moment, and tried to absorb everything I'd learned. The death chart was telling me that it was my destiny to learn painful life lessons through my relationship with my mother and her loss. Karma was at work here.

I felt a vast relief, seeing that. It changed my view of my mother in so many ways. We had been incarnated together in this lifetime to learn things from each other, and neither was really a victim or victor. I folded the chart to fit in my bag, organized my papers for the next day, and headed home. That night, a full moon lunar eclipse would be visible across most of the U.S. For an astrologer, any eclipse was worth watching, and although I'd be watching alone, I thought back to six years earlier, when Della had joined me to watch a different lunar eclipse.

The nights had started to get cool, but late season summer flowers still bloomed in the garden. We'd settled into the chairs and watched the last pink sunset clouds fade into gray as the moon moved higher in the sky. Incrementally, its disk darkened and the shadow across it became a bite of blackness. Della had been spellbound and amazed. Their eyes in the dimming light shone bright with intelligence, as their long, wavy hair tumbled past their shoulders. I remembered leaning over and kissing Della's fore-head—their arms came around my neck to hug me—and wishing I had memories of sharing something special like this with my mother.*

Once the eclipse passed totality, I returned indoors, still thinking about my mother and her chart with the tense grand cross. I took it to bed with me, arranged my pillows, and looked at the symbols once again. The wounded healer, Chiron, was in a love-hate relationship with Saturn, the planet of karma. Karma meant Mom's illness was part of her soul's journey, not a random event. Although others might not believe this, I did, completely. Especially when the planets confirmed it. I studied the chart some more, enjoying the quiet of the house at this hour, listening to Mindy beside me turning pages in the book she was reading. I loved my family so much, and that love was giving me the strength to look deeper into my mom's life.

I saw that one of the main planets, Pluto, lord of the underworld, was conjoined on the chart with Uranus. This combination signaled unpredictability around Mom's death, which made sense: even as she knew it was coming, Mom had been surprised by the fast descent. I remembered Lou Ann telling me about our mother sobbing one night, hearing her say over and over she didn't want to die. Both my parents must have seen the looming shadow approach, even though they kept us in the dark.

I yawned. It was late and tomorrow would be a busy day. But as I gave the chart one last scan, I saw what I'd been searching for: the moon's nodes lined up with the symbols for parents in my chart. According to the death chart for my mother, my own time for having parents was over. It was eerie but accurate.

Mindy set her book down and gave me a kiss. "I hope you're finding some peace from that work tonight," she said.

I nodded. I certainly had. Some of my questions had been answered. Not all, but some.

---

*Della uses the pronouns *they, them, theirs.*

52

A Twin's Chart

A few weeks later, the question I'd been dreading appeared in my email. A twin wanted to know why her sister died, not her. I almost pressed delete, but I made myself stop. Earlier, I had promised myself: no death chart readings for twins. What if I broke down during the session, losing all objectivity? I prided myself on professionalism, the distance that made a good astrologer. So many years ago, my teacher Zip encouraged me to maintain objectivity while staying warm and friendly, and my coworker in the Sunsight bookstore helped me to avoid taking on others' energy so I could stay healthy.

I turned from my desk and went over to the shelf where Lou Ann's raku pot sat, a reminder of my sister's creativity and eye for beauty. I sat, cradling it in both hands, thinking about how lonely I had been in the beginning, how I'd gotten so much help from countless people along the way: Gayle, the homeopath, other Twinless twins, and even myself. Lou Ann had been gone for almost twelve years now. Maybe I was strong enough to face others who had a similar loss, to help them as I'd been helped. I called Christine to set up a session for early the following week.

By the time I got home, the September day had turned cool. Ana sat at the dining room table, textbooks spread around, music blaring from her iPod's speakers. Thunder clapped in the distance, and through the rattling screen door gusts of rain-scented wind blew in. I tapped my daughter on the shoulder. "I need help closing windows." We watched a thick sheet of rain approach as we frantically got the downstairs windows shut and then raced for the upstairs ones.

Mindy pushed in the back door, soaking wet. I handed her a dry towel. Lightning flashed in a dark sky, followed by a loud clap overhead.

"Glad you're home."

"Me too." She wiped her face and hands, and hung the towel on a hook. "I'm going to put on dry clothes."

I started slicing cucumbers for a salad as the room grew darker and rain pounded the closed windows. Midwestern thunderstorms happened predictably in summer and fall, but each one startled me with its power. Lightning flashed, thunder boomed, and suddenly a loud thud shook the house. The lights went off.

"Ema!" Ana called. I dropped my knife and ran to the back window where she stood. "Look!"

Our home was graced by old oak trees, the pride of our St. Paul neighborhood. We loved those trees, depended on them for shade during the hot weather, worried about them when the winter storms came. One of our hundred-year-old red oaks lay uprooted, the power lines tangled around it. It had landed on the neighbor's garage, crushing the roof and siding.

Mindy hurried over. "What happened?" She put her hand on my shoulder as we peered through the blinding rain at the horizontal tree. "Oh no," she said. "I loved that tree."

For two days, our power was out. We made endless phone calls, ate takeout, and went to bed early, reading by flashlight. Ana even thought it was fun, a bit like camping. One morning, I woke up and realized it was the day of Christine's reading. I'd been so occupied with living off the grid that I'd almost forgotten.

Even though the day was warm, Christine pulled her cardigan closed as we sat down in my office. Remembering what I'd learned about listening, I started with a question. "I'd like to hear how your sister died, if you want to talk about it."

She sighed and folded her hands in her lap. Her long brown hair was pulled back into a bun with barrettes on both sides, and I wondered if her twin had looked like her. "She got breast cancer, the aggressive kind. Only lived a year after her diagnosis." She pulled the edges of her sweater closer. "I went to New Jersey to stay with her for the last month. She didn't want to talk about it, but we both knew she was dying." Christine looked away. "On her last night, she begged me to crawl into bed with her. I held her hand as she took her last breath."

Oh, this was hard. I gave myself a minute, pretending to study her chart while the tremors inside calmed. How clearly I remembered crawling into bed with Lou Ann during those last hours of her life, trying to infuse her dying body with my own warmth. I took a sip of water and cleared my throat, hoping my voice wouldn't shake. "How are you now?"

"I'm sad, but doing better than I expected. I'm surprised." She shrugged. "So, tell me about this death chart. What did you learn about us?"

I'd done charts for both twins to understand them better, and though they were born eleven minutes apart, those few minutes made a specific difference. I'd seen two extremely sensitive people, but Christine's sensitivity was offset by planets grounded in earth houses, a big contrast to her sister's. That made all the difference in both their lives and deaths. When I shared this with Christine, she nodded.

"I was the one who plodded along and did what needed to be done," she said. "I had a family of my own to look after. Then I took care of our mom when she got ill. My twin never married. She moved to the east coast and struggled with anxiety and depression most of her adult life."

Lou Ann and I looked alike, spoke alike, and thought alike. High school friends would call the house and guess which one of us had answered. One boy asked if he could date both of us to decide who he liked better. Sometimes I would ask Mom a question, and a moment later Lou Ann would enter the room and ask the exact same question. Other times I would get an exciting idea for a school project, and Lou Ann's would be nearly identical, even though we hadn't compared notes. I loved seeing myself mirrored in my twin this way, but I also wanted to be my own person. The fact was I didn't really know who I was without my sister. Starting in childhood, she was the strong, capable one, acting in the role of parent after Mom died. We never managed to undo that conditioning. I compared myself to her, and most often got the short end of the stick. As we grew up together, I could only remember a few times she failed to be the leader in our little band of two.

When we were sixteen, Dad took us for our driver's tests. Both of us had struggled to learn parallel parking, but on the day of the test our heavy station wagon seemed to slide perfectly into place for me. Lou Ann knocked over a couple of cones, and that was enough for her to fail.

Standing alone and relying only on myself didn't happen completely until after Lou Ann's death. In navigating both Henrietta's and Dad's illnesses without Lou Ann, when I made medical decisions, arranged for changes in their care, and helped take care of financial decisions, I learned to trust myself without hesitation. I didn't need Lou Ann's advice or coaching; I did a good job on my own.

Lou Ann's and my charts were more alike than Christine's and her twin's, yet we also took on different roles in our lives. Lou Ann had conformed to more family expectations and given the appearance of being strong and together, while outwardly I appeared to struggle more. But I was more grounded in many ways, even though I'd broken with family tradition by choosing astrology. Christine's sister's death had come at a time when Christine experienced an eclipse, or shadow on her sun, the symbol of identity, while Uranus activated her Moon, a symbol for belonging, intimacy, and family. Her sense of being known and understood by another person would never be the same. *How delicate the balance of life and death*, I thought, as I gathered my papers after she left.

I knew crews were working on our power and ready to cut the limbs of the fallen tree for removal. I'd seen a truck that morning. When I got home that afternoon the last of it was gone. Only a long dark gash marked its passing in our garden. I wondered what we'd do with the big stump left behind.

53

Underwater

Death chart work was now keeping me even busier at work. But I'd committed months ago to a march to raise research money for ovarian cancer. It was hard to arrive that sunny October day and see the women waiting to walk, many with scarves covering chemo-bald heads, some as painfully thin as Lou Ann had been during her treatment.

I picked up my banner at the registration table and nearly bumped into one of them. She was sobbing in her husband's arms, her hands covering her face. "I can't do it," she cried. "I have to go home. I'm too nauseous." Her words, the oversized jacket, and her stocking cap brought back a flood of memories: an overdressed Lou Ann in the front seat of my car telling me, "Life is for the living." Even though she'd insisted on surgery two days later, I knew part of her had already given up. I could only imagine what the woman and her family were going through. Trips to their clinic, unending nausea and other side effects. Cancer hurt everyone in a family, not just the person who was ill. I wanted to hold out my arms and take this woman into them, but instead I turned from the table and looked for Mindy and the kids.

What a silent killer ovarian cancer was, known for having few symptoms until it advanced too far to treat effectively. My research, all those years ago, had told me only half of all those diagnosed survived beyond five years, and that was with early diagnosis, before it spread, which was only 15 percent of cases. I watched the sobbing woman, her husband, and her boys move off toward the parking lot, and my heart ached.

Lou Ann hadn't wanted to know what I found on the internet. I didn't blame her, guessing that deep inside she already knew. That week after her surgery, when the lab results came in, her prognosis was bleak. I remembered four different studies saying the survival rate for her type of ovarian cancer was 1 percent.

She'd eaten well that morning; she was sitting at the kitchen table sipping tea when I arrived, pointing to her empty plate. "I ate two eggs and a piece of toast for breakfast," she said, pride in her voice, wanting to show me how alert and healthy she was despite the numbers, "and I already know what I want for lunch." But when I tried to tell her about my research, she shook her head. "I don't want to know what you learned," she said. "Let's enjoy the moment."

We'd tried to. I'd given it my best shot. But her death hung over us both, like the shadow I'd seen on my mother's chart, and neither of us could ignore it.

Della came running toward me waving a bottle of water. Ana was right behind them, eating a banana. They'd been to the food tent. Ana grabbed my hand as Mindy joined us, and we walked toward the group by the lake. I handed Mindy the banner to pin on the back of my shirt. "In honor of Lou Ann Lewis," it read.

This walk was easier than the Rocky Mountain hike we'd taken where we'd seen the elk, but it was equally meaningful to me. After a few minutes, the pack moved ahead and I was with just Mindy and the kids. The sun sparkled on the pond, and red-orange leaves fluttered in the breeze. Overhead stretched a brilliant October sky, and when I heard a Canada goose honk, I looked up to see the familiar V-shaped formation flying south. Like the position of the stars, it was something I could count on.

We circled the lake one time, a total of one and a half miles. I was sore from my surgery, but I made it with my family's help and their tolerance for my slow pace. Just a week earlier, I'd gone through surgery to have my ovaries removed, agreeing with the advice of the genetics counselor—my way of guaranteeing I'd never get the same disease as my twin. Completing the walk felt like a marker in some way, and I sensed Lou Ann's presence the entire time.

Part of my mind, though, was on the next day. Sandra, a new client, was coming to see me only six weeks after her daughter Erin had been killed. Losing a child was the worst thing I could imagine, even worse than losing a twin. I watched Ana and Della run ahead, their long hair catching light from the sun, their laughter growing fainter as they sped ahead. Erin and Della were almost the same age. What could I possibly say to this grieving mother?

I TOOK ERIN's death chart out of the printer. I'd only worked with Sandra once before Erin's death, and I liked her quiet energy. She had called me about Erin, hardly able to speak clearly on the phone, and I knew the shock and confusion about losing her daughter would be a big part of our session. Death charts were important to me because of Lou Ann, but as soon as I began doing them I sensed they had a deeper service. If someone could be reassured about the reason for a death, as seen in the charts, and know aspects of this mystery as best as I could read them, perhaps their suffering would be eased. That had happened with the few readings I'd done in the last few months, and I felt grateful to have this new tool to offer those left behind.

On Erin's chart, Mars and Uranus were prominent, indicating an accident that was quick and, with the unpredictable energy of Uranus that I'd also noticed in my mom's chart, unexpected. From reading the chart, I was certain Erin didn't suffer. That was a relief, something I could pass on to Sandra to ease her heart. Each death chart also has the symbols for others in the person's close orbit, especially family. I noticed the symbol for her mom, the moon, was conjunct to Neptune, the psychic planet. Both planets were rising. To others looking at the chart, this might mean nothing. To a professional astrologer, the symbolism was clear. At the moment of her death, Erin had tried to send her mom a message through intuitive channels. She wanted her mom to know she'd gone into the light. This realization brought goosebumps. It gave me a clear way to bring peace and understanding to Sandra.

Erin had been spending part of her junior year of high school in Spain, and she was sightseeing with friends in a small village when she was struck by a car. Sandra told me the driver had a heart attack. "The authorities said Erin died instantly," Sandra said, looking out my office window from her place on my green couch. "One of her friends told me Erin came to her in a dream and apologized for ruining everyone's plans. That's the kind of kid she was."

"Did you notice or feel anything different on the day she died?" I asked, thinking of Erin's chart, the symbols of a message coming to her mother. "Before you were notified?"

"In fact, I did." Sandra ran her fingers through her short hair. "I was underwater all day, like I couldn't wake up. Every action took enormous effort. I never felt like that before."

"Maybe your body already knew before you got the news?"

She sat up straight. "That's exactly right." Tears leaked down her solemn face. "I miss her terribly. She was a truly good human being. But somehow, I know she's OK. That brings me peace."

When I walked up to our house that evening, the smell of freshly cut wood was overpowering. In place of the oak tree's stump was a pile of sawdust. Mindy had arranged for the tree stump to be ground out, and now almost every vestige of the beautiful oak that had shaded our yard was gone.

I couldn't help but think of Sandra, how her life had changed in an instant. She would never see or talk to her daughter again. We needed to savor the presence of the people we loved in our lives, not take them for granted, not even for a moment. I hurried inside to hug and kiss my children and Mindy.

54

The Conference

The jagged red rocks just outside of Zion National Park glowed in the morning sun as I walked to the hotel classroom. I'd become a fan of Utah a few years earlier, after one of our best family vacations that included some spectacular stargazing just north of here. The dry air and smell of pungent sage was like a soothing balm. As I walked into the building, I fingered the smooth rose quartz crystal in my pocket. A gift from Lou Ann during her last days of life, it always calmed me, but today I held it tight.

Thirty minutes later, I stood in front of the darkened room full of one hundred astrologers from all over the world, including a dozen or so colleagues I respected and loved beyond measure. As my PowerPoint presentation lit up the screen behind me, I took a deep breath. I remembered the first time I'd looked at Lou Ann's death chart and wondered how I would ever make sense of it.

"Today I'll be talking about using the death chart as a tool to counsel the bereaved. First, though, I want to tell you how I came to study death charts." I shifted my weight from foot to foot as I continued. "Because my identical twin and I were born together, I always assumed we'd die together. I took for granted that we'd be together always. Life without her was unimaginable." I saw heads nodding around the room. "Unfortunately, that was not the case. She died in 2005, and it was the study of a chart cast at the moment of her death, a death chart, that helped me make sense of my loss." As I put my hand in my pocket, I imaged Lou Ann sending me a message of support and love through the rose crystal.

"Grief hurts. It's a deep, searing, visceral hurt, and it's a natural human response to avoid pain. But there is no healing from grief without going through the pain. You have to feel it." As I took a moment to breathe, I remembered the deep emptiness inside me after Lou Ann's death. "Healing happens on the other side."

I paused to compose myself. "A major loss can cause all kinds of additional troubles. Trouble sleeping, overeating, undereating, alcohol and drug use, physical ailments, recklessness, apathy, and overworking are among the most common coping mechanisms."

I continued by talking about how using the death chart could connect the loved ones to the experience of the person who had died. "The chart is a road map to the minutes before, during, and after the moment of death. It can also show the bereaved what lessons are there to take away from the experience." I knew that Uranus, the planet of individuation, was my major teacher in Lou Ann's death chart. And here I stood, without Lou Ann for twelve years now, as one of the first astrologers to bring this unique tool to light.

I went through examples of death charts, explaining the significant astrological features and sharing the knowledge I'd gained in working with nearly forty clients who'd brought death charts to me. Every session I'd had was pure discovery. Not only did the chart describe the situation surrounding the person's death, but each client, hearing their experience validated, seemed to relax and change right in front of me.

As I let that thought sink in with the audience, I remembered the day that Max came in for a session. Max and his now late mentor had run a chiropractic school and clinic together for a dozen years. The clinic had money problems, and his mentor had personal problems, which ended in his suicide. I knew suicide was among the most difficult of deaths to accept, but I also knew Max was deeply spiritual.

"Look at the eclipse," I said, holding the paper so Max could see the symbol for his spiritual path being activated. "Everything in this death chart says that he'd taken the business as far as he could and it was time for a change."

Max sighed. "I knew deep inside that it was my time to step up. I had no idea that would happen like this." He took a deep breath, and I could see him fill up with energy. "After he died, I started to transcribe his notes. That forced me to realize how much I'd learned. It gave me confidence to carry on his work." He caught my eyes. "I never thought he might really be done with his part of the work."

The memory faded as I looked at my watch. "I'm almost out of time, so in conclusion I want to remind you that death records are open to the public. If you've lost someone you love, find their time of death and cast a chart. It may help you, and working with these is just one more tool we have as astrologers to help bring meaning to people's lives."

The lights came up as I was thanking everyone for their attention. I grabbed my flash drive from the computer and walked back to my seat. Someone commented on how well I'd done, but what really mattered was the warmth I felt from the quartz emanating through my clothes.

Barb pulled me aside at the break. She was one of the trusted colleagues who had helped me come to terms with Lou Ann's impending death. "I learned something important from your talk today. After my first husband died, my only daughter from that marriage went off the rails. She was almost thirty years old at the time." Barb tugged on the silk scarf around her neck. "He and I were only married four years, and I figured out marrying him was a mistake pretty early on." She repositioned the scarf. "This daughter had always been so easy, a rule follower and a conformist. After her dad died, she started drinking, got a couple DWIs, and was completely out of control for a while." The lights in the room flashed, signaling that another lecture was about to begin. "It never occurred to me, since I was completely finished with her dad, that those were grief responses." She patted my arm. "I understand now."

After one more presentation on astronomy, we took a break for lunch. As I was walking back from lunch with a couple of friends, a young dark-haired woman came up to me. "Can I talk to you?" She held her hands together so tightly her knuckles looked white.

"Of course." I turned to my friends. "See you inside."

"I'm an identical twin." She said. Suddenly the tension in her posture made sense. "I have to ask. Can you tell from looking at the charts which twin will live longer?"

I took a deep breath. "I'm sorry. I made you think about losing your twin, didn't I?"

"Yes." Her eyes grew moist as she looked away.

"I don't think there's a way to tell when someone will die from their chart. It's a map of potentials, not outcomes."

THE CONFERENCE WAS over, and a group of us were waiting for the van to transport us to the airport. I felt deeply satisfied with the connections I'd made, the new astrology I'd learned, and the response to my presentation. I was eager to get home to Mindy and talk in person with her about how well things had gone. Two people had signed up for death charts on the spot. Only one thing bothered me. Was part of my new role to be the person who forced other twins to think about losing each other? My hope was to serve as an example of moving through loss to life.

A voice interrupted my thoughts. "Can I have your card?" a woman in a bright, flowered blouse asked. I'd been in a breakout group with her earlier in the day. "I'm the president of our local chapter of NCGR [National Council for Geocosmic Research] in Las Vegas, and I'd like you to come speak on death charts to our group. We can't pay much, but I know the leaders of groups in Phoenix and Tucson. We can help you work out the timing so you can to speak at all of them, and it might be worth a trip."

"That sounds great. It's an easy trip from the Twin Cities to both Phoenix and Las Vegas." I fished out my business card. "Let's email in the next couple of weeks."

55

Screaming with Delight

Bright pinks and soft purples streaked the sky as the clouds reflected the setting sun through the windows of the Campus Club at the University of Minnesota. Mindy invited me to join her at an event to support one of the local food movements, WEI (Women's Environmental Institute). Bursts of bright laughter mixed with the chattering sounds as groups of people snaked through a long line to the buffet table, waiting to fill their plates with locally sourced food and cider.

"How are you?" a woman touched my shoulder. "It's me, Suzanne."

"Wow, Sue, it's been almost twenty years. How are you?" Over two decades ago Sue was a client who referred many of her psychotherapy patients to me. I still felt gratitude when I remembered the breadth of her support. She moved out of state, and we gradually lost touch.

"I saw you at Elizabeth's house after Lou Ann died, remember?"

"Sorry, that period of time is pretty fuzzy." I was slightly alarmed that I had no memory of seeing her at all, but lately I'd discovered there were many things from that time period I couldn't remember.

"Well, how are you?"

"I'm great."

And as I said the words, I realized it was the truth. I laughed at the dinner table with Mindy and the kids over our silly in-jokes, felt excitement about my new astrology work, and appreciated my good health daily. After Lou Ann died, I feared all of that had left my world forever.

Walking back to our table with the sweetness of cider and squash wafting up from my plate, I glanced out the windows, where wispy vermilion clouds lightened a darkening sky. I pulled in my chair next to Mindy, who leaned in close and squeezed my arm. "I'm glad you decided to come tonight," she said.

Later, when we got home, Della sat stretched out on the couch, their open computer on their lap, messaging friends while they watched TV. They looked up. "How was your event?" In that moment I realized how close Della was to adulthood. Soon they would graduate high school and move away to college.

"It was lovely," I said.

"Ana's in bed, but she wants to see you."

Mindy sat down next to Della, and I heard their soft voices as I walked up the stairs. Ana sat propped up with pillows, reading a teen magazine. "Did you know that Selena Gomez answers every piece of fan mail?" Her brown eyes twinkled. "I'm writing her tomorrow."

I leaned over and kissed her cheek. "I'm sure you will. Lights out in ten."

Grief still touched me in lonely moments when no one understood me the way Lou Ann could, or when I desperately needed to fill in the blanks of childhood memories. Also in happy moments when Ana chanted Torah at her bat mitzvah or Della discussed their college choices. I longed for Lou Ann to be at these markers and turning points of my life and my family's life, but that dream was gone. Instead, I'd hold the smooth rose quartz or her raku pot with the heart on top and feel her close. Sometimes I'd remember her final breath, but that scene most often reminded me of the two us of standing under a small ledge in Glacier National Park screaming with delight during a hailstorm.

As word about my work with death charts traveled around the globe, and people from Spain and Australia called for sessions, I saw how Lou Ann's death had started me down a new path. Without her death, there would be no original chart to study. There would have been no need to find meaning in my journey through grief, and no way to help others with their losses. At night, I'd look up to see Orion in a winter sky, or Castor and Pollux in the summer sky, and be reminded that Lou Ann and I were connected to the same cosmos.

I realized that blessings had come to me after Mom died. It took me many years to see how her death brought an unexpected liberation. Of course I missed Mom, and I missed Lou Ann beyond words. But letting them go also meant I could let myself grow into who I really am. Mom's constant criticism, shame, and harshness had hurt me, but her early death had liberated me from more of the same and allowed me to search for myself. I wondered at times how she would have responded to my lesbianism; I'd known other Jewish women whose families said the mourner's kaddish for them when they came out, effectively breaking family bonds forever. Being a professional astrologer would not have garnered praise from Mom either, but I could imagine her coming to accept it. Would I have pursued these two aspects of myself, so vital to me now, if she'd lived?

I never imagined losing Lou Ann would bring liberation, but it did. All my twin ever did was support and love me, but comparison was part of our lives, as it is for all twins. It seemed to be woven into the fabric of our being. Once Lou Ann was gone, all my comparisons left with her, as if the huge thunderstorm that roared through St. Paul as she took her final breath washed them away. In their place emerged an individual. There was no one to mirror my looks, my thoughts, or my actions. They became mine alone.

At times, I clung to a silk jacket Lou Ann gave me, some earrings we shared, or the pots shaped by her hands, thinking these were what was left of her, until enough time passed for me to realize my sister's parting gift to me was the death chart. A small piece of paper with symbols and patterns that revealed meaning, and changed an unfair, unthinkable loss to something meaningful. Her chart taught me she had fulfilled her purpose here on Earth; she'd completed her cycle. My clients' charts also showed me how death might be a spiritual decision, a way for them to move further on their soul's journey.

Lou Ann's ending was my beginning. Grief started me on a new path, and it took me to very unexpected places. Through grief, I learned another way to carry forward my twin's love of helping people. And I increased my capacity for understanding the language of the stars.

Acknowledgments

My heartfelt thanks to my writing teacher and coach, Mary Carroll Moore, and the wonderful writers in her classes who sent thoughtful, loving feedback week after week: Shelley Jerige, Yvette Lewis, Mary Kipp, and Cherste Eidman.

My deep thanks to the people who supported Lou Ann through her illness: Elizabeth, her care team, and her larger community. There are too many to name, but you know who you are.

Also, to those who helped me through the horrific time after her death: Gayle Sherman Crandell, Ariella Tilsen, Shir Tikvah members, Judy Kurzer and Amy Kurzer, the late Leonore Kurzer, Susan Sobelson, Judith Ingram, Debbie Zelle, and Mary Gooch.

My profound gratitude to my beta readers and those who read the book to write endorsements: Janice Friedman, Shelley Jerige, Yvette Lewis, Akane Little, Susan Sobelson, Jacqueline White, Linda Pountney, Gayle Crandell, Arlan Wise, Alison Bechdel, and Beth Zemsky.

For her skill and expertise in managing the production of the book, Beth Wright; the beautiful book cover, Christian Fuenfhausen; the great promotional advice, Scott Edelstein and Rachel Greenhouse.

And most of all, for all their love and safe harbor, Mindy, Della, and Ana.